CREATION
AND ITS RECORDS

B.H. Baden-Powell

Creation and Its Records

B.H. Baden-Powell

© 1st World Library – Literary Society, 2004
PO Box 2211
Fairfield, IA 52556
www.1stworldlibrary.org
First Edition

LCCN: 2005901134

Softcover ISBN: 1-4218-1112-X
Hardcover ISBN: 1-4218-1012-3
eBook ISBN: 1-4218-1212-6

Purchase *"Creation and Its Record"*
as a traditional bound book at:
www.1stWorldLibrary.org/purchase.asp?ISBN=1-4218-1112-X

1st World Library Literary Society is a nonprofit organization dedicated to promoting literacy by:

- Creating a free internet library accessible from any computer worldwide.
- Hosting writing competitions and offering book publishing scholarships.

Readers interested in supporting literacy through sponsorship, donations or membership please contact:
literacy@1stworldlibrary.org
Check us out at: www.classiclibrary.ORG
and start downloading free ebooks today.

Creation and Its Records
contributed by Tim, Ed & Rodney
in support of
1st World Library Literary Society

CONTENTS

PART I.

I. INTRODUCTORY 7

II. THE ELEMENT OF *FAITH* IN CREATION 17

III. THE DOCTRINE OF CREATION STATED 23

IV. CREATIVE DESIGN IN INORGANIC MATTER 32

V. THE CREATION OF LIVING MATTER 42

VI. THE MARKS OF CREATIVE INTELLIGENCE IN THE EVOLUTION OF ORGANIC FORMS 53

VII. THE DESCENT OF MAN 74

VIII. FURTHER DIFFICULTIES REGARDING THE HISTORY OF MAN 93

IX. CONCLUDING REMARKS 105

PART II.

X. THE GENESIS NARRATIVE - ITS IMPORTANCE 110

XI. SCRIPTURE METHODS OF REVELATION 119

XII. METHODS OF INTERPRETING THE NARRATIVE - ASSUMPTIONS OF MEANING TO CERTAIN TERMS 128

XIII. THE GENESIS NARRATIVE CONSIDERED
GENERALLY 132
(I.) THE FIRST PART OF THE NARRATIVE 132
(II.) THE SECOND PART 135

XIV. THE INTERPRETATION SUPPORTED BY
OTHER SCRIPTURES 148

XV. AND SUPPORTED BY THE CONTEXT 153

XVI. THE DETAILS OF THE CREATION
NARRATIVE 161

APPENDIX.

PROFESSOR DELITZSCH ON THE
GARDEN OF EDEN 187

PART I

CHAPTER I.

INTRODUCTORY

Among the recollections that are lifelong, I have one as vivid as ever after more than twenty-five years have elapsed; it is of an evening lecture - the first of a series - given at South Kensington to working men. The lecturer was Professor Huxley; his subject, the Common Lobster. All the apparatus used was a good-sized specimen of the creature itself, a penknife, and a black-board and chalk. With such materials the professor gave us not only an exposition, matchless in its lucidity, of the structure of the crustacea, but such an insight into the purposes and methods of biological study as few could in those days have anticipated. For there were as yet no Science Primers, no International Series; and the "new biology" came upon us like the revelation of another world. I think that lecture gave me, what I might otherwise never have got (and what some people never get), a profound conviction of the reality and meaning of facts in nature. That impression I have brought to the attempt which this little book embodies. The facts of nature are God's revelation, of the same weight, though not the same in kind, as His written Word.

At the same time, the further conviction is strong in my mind, not merely of the obvious truth that the Facts and the Writing (if both genuine) cannot really differ, but further, that there must be, after all, a true way of explaining the Writing, if only it is looked for carefully - a way that will surmount not only the difficulty of the subject, but also the impatience with which some will regard the attempt. Like so many other questions connected with religion, the question of reconciliation produces its double effect. People will ridicule attempts to solve it, but all the same they will return again and again to the task of its actual solution.

That the latter part of the proposition is true, has recently received illustration in the fact that a review like the *Nineteenth Century*, which has so little space to spare, has found room in four successive numbers[1] for articles by Gladstone, Huxley, and H. Drummond, on the subject of "Creation and its Records." May I make one remark on this interesting science tournament? I can understand the scientific conclusions Professor Huxley has given us. I can also understand Mr. Gladstone, because he values the Writing as the professor values the Facts. But one thing I can *not* understand. Why is Professor Huxley so angry or so contemptuous with people who value the Bible, whole and as it stands, and want to see its accuracy vindicated? Why are they fanatics, Sisyphus-labourers, and what not? That they are a very large group numerically, and hardly contemptible intellectually, is, I think, obvious; that a further large group (who would not identify themselves wholly with the out-and-out Bible defenders) feel a certain amount of sympathy, is proved by the interest taken in the controversy. Yet all "reconcilers" are ridiculed or denounced - at any rate are contemptuously dismissed. Can it be that the professor has for the moment overlooked one very simple fact?

The great bulk of those interested in the question place their whole hope for their higher moral and spiritual life in this world and the next on one central Person - the LORD JESUS CHRIST. If He is wrong, then no one can be right - there is no such thing as right: that is what they feel. It will be conceded that it is hardly "fanatical" to feel this. But if so, surely it is not fanatical, but agreeable to the soberest reason, further to hold that this (to them sacred) PERSON did (and His apostles with Him) treat the Book of Genesis as a whole (and not merely parts of it) as a genuine revelation - or, to use the popular expression, as the *Word of* GOD. That being so, can it be matter for surprise or contemptuous pity, that they should be anxious to vindicate the Book, to be satisfied that the MASTER was not wrong? That is the ultimate and very real issue involved in the question of Genesis.

As long as people feel *that*, they must seek the reconciliation of the two opposing ideas. If the attempt is made in a foolish or bitter spirit, or without a candid appreciation of the facts, then the attempt will no doubt excite just displeasure. But need it always be so made?

As to the first part of my proposition that attempts to reconcile religion and science are received with a certain dislike, it is due partly to the unwisdom with which they are sometimes made. Prof. H. Drummond speaks of the dislike as general.[1]

If this is so, I, as a "reconciler," can only ask for indulgence, hoping that grace may be extended to me on the ground of having something to say on the subject that has not yet been considered.

Nor, as regards the impatience of the public, can I admit that there is only fault on one side. In the first place, it will not be denied that some writers, delighted with the vast, and apparently boundless, vision that the discovery (in its modern form) of Evolution opened out to them, did incautiously proceed, while surveying their new kingdom, to assert for it bounds that stretch beyond its legitimate scope.

Religionists, on the other hand, imagining, however wrongly, that the erroneous extension was part of the true scientific doctrine, attacked the whole without discrimination.

While such a misapprehension existed, it was inevitable that writers anxious alike for the dignity of science and the maintenance of religion, should step in to point out the error, and effect a reconciliation of claims which really were never in conflict.

It is hardly the fault of "religionists" that it was at first supposed that one *could* not hold the doctrine of evolution without denying a "special" creation and a designing Providence. It was on this very natural supposition that the first leading attack - attributed to the Bishop of Oxford - proceeded. And the writer fell into the equally natural mistake of taking advantage of the uncompleted and unproved state of the theory at the time, to attack the theory itself, instead of keeping to the safer ground, namely, that whatever might ultimately be the conclusion of evolutionists, it was quite certain that no theory of evolution that at all coincided with the known facts, offered any ground for argument against the existence of an Intelligent

Lawgiver and First Cause of all; nor did it tend in the slightest to show that no such thing as creative design and providence existed in the course of nature.

What the discovery of evolution really did, was to necessitate a revision of the hitherto popularly accepted and generally assumed and unquestioned notion of what *creation* was. And it has long appeared to me, that while now the most thoroughgoing advocates of evolution generally admit that their justly cherished doctrine has nothing to say to the existence of a Creator, or to the possibility of design - which may be accepted or denied on other grounds - the writers on the side of Christianity have not sufficiently recognized the change which their views ought to undergo.

As long as this is the case, there will continue to be a certain "conflict," not indeed between science and religion, but of the kind which has been vividly depicted by the late Dr. Draper.

It can scarcely have escaped the notice of the most ordinary reader that, in the course of that interesting work, the author has very little to say about religion - at any rate about religion in any proper sense of the term. The conflict was between a Church which had a zeal for God without knowledge, and the progress of scientific thought; it was also a conflict between discovered facts, and facts which existed, not in the Bible, but in a particular interpretation, however generally received, of it.

The present work is therefore addressed primarily to Christian believers who still remain perplexed as to what they ought to believe; and its aim is to prevent, if may be, an unreasonable alarm at, and a useless opposition to, the conclusions of modern science; while, at the same time, it tells them in simple language how far those conclusions really go, and how very groundless is the fear that they will ever subvert a true faith that, antecedent to the most wonderful chain of causation and methodical working which science can establish, there is still a Divine Designer - One who upholds all things "by the word of His power."

The doctrine of evolution is still the *ignotum* to a great many, and it is therefore, according to the time-honoured proverb, taken *pro magnifico*, as something terribly adverse to the faith. Nor can it be fairly denied, as I before remarked, that some of the students of the theory have become so enamoured of it, so carried away by the intoxication of the gigantic speculation it opens out to the imagination, that they have succumbed to the temptation to carry speculation beyond what the proof warrants, and thus lend some aid to the deplorable confusion, which would blend in one, what is legitimate inference and what is unproved hypothesis or mere supposition.

It only remains to say that the basis of this little book is a short course of lectures in which I endeavoured to disarm the prejudices of an educated but not scientifically critical audience, by simply stating how far the theory of cosmical evolution had been really proved - proved, that is, to the extent of that reasonable certainty which satisfies the ordinary "prudent man" in affairs of weight and importance. I have tried to show that evolution, apart from fanciful and speculative extensions of it, allows, if it does not directly establish, that the operation of nature is not a chance or uncontrolled procedure, but one that suggests a distinct set of lines, and an orderly obedience to pre-conceived law, intelligently and beneficently (in the end) designed.

There are obviously two main points which the Christian reader requires to have made clear. The first is that, the modern theory of evolution being admitted, the constitution of matter in the universe and the principles of development in organic life, which that theory establishes, not only do not exclude, but positively demand, the conception of a Divine artificer and director. The second point, which is perhaps of still greater weight with the believer, is that where revelation (which is his ultimate standard of appeal) has touched upon the subject of creation, its statements are not merely a literary fancy, an imaginary cosmogony, false in its facts though enshrining Divine truth, but are as a whole perfectly true.

Whatever novelty there may be, is to be found in the treatment of the second subject. The first portion of the work is only a brief and popular statement of facts, quite unnecessary to the scientific reader but probably very necessary to the large body of Churchmen, who have not studied science, but are quite able to appreciate scientific fact and its bearings when placed before them in an untechnical form, and divested of needless details and subordinate questions.

But it is around the supposed declarations of Scripture on the subject of creation that the real "conflict" has centred. Let us look the matter quite fairly in the face. We accept the conclusion that (let us say) the horse was developed and gradually perfected or advanced to his present form and characteristics, by a number of stages, and that it took a very long time to effect this result. Now, if there is anywhere a statement in Holy Writ that (*a*) a horse was *per saltum* called into existence in a distinctive and complete form, by a special creative *fiat*, and that (*b*) this happened not gradually, but in a limited and specified moment of time, then I will at once admit that the record (assuming that its meaning is not to be mistaken) is not provably right, if it is not clearly wrong; and accept the consequences, momentous as they would be. If, in the same way, the Record asserts that man, or at least man the direct progenitor of the Semitic race,[1] was a distinct and special creation, his bodily frame having some not completely explained developmental connection with the animal creation, but his higher nature being imparted as a special and unique creative endowment out of the line of physical development altogether, then I shall accept the Record, because the proved facts of science have nothing to say against it, whatever Drs. Buchner, Vogt, Haeckel, and others may assert to the contrary.

In the first of my two instances, the popular idea has long been that the sacred record *does* say something about a direct and separate creative act; and this idea has been the origin and ground of all the supposed conflict between science and "religion." As long as this idea continues, it can hardly be said that a book addressed to the clearing up of the subject is unnecessary or to be rejected *per se*.

As to the method in which this subject will be dealt with, I shall maintain that the Scripture does *not* say anything about the horse, or the whale, or the ox, or any other animal, being separately or directly created. And the view thus taken of the Record I have not met with before. This it is necessary to state, not because the fact would lend any value to the interpretation - rather the contrary; but because it justifies me in submitting what, if new, may be intrinsically important, to the judgment of the Church; and it also protects me from the offence of plagiarism, however unwitting. If others have thought out the same rendering of the Genesis history, so much the better for my case; but what is here set down occurred to me quite independently.

A study of the real meaning of the Record, in the light of what may be fairly regarded as proved facts, cannot be without its use to the Christian. If it be true that a certain amount of information on the subject of creation is contained in revelation, it must have been so contained for a specific purpose - a purpose to be attained at some stage or other of the history of mankind. It is possible also that the study will bring to light a probable, or at any rate a possible, explanation of some of those apparent (if they are not real) "deadlocks" which occur in pursuing the course of life history on the earth.

Such considerations will naturally have more weight with the Christian believer than with those who reject the faith. But at least the advantage of them remains with the believer, till the contrary is shown. The extreme evolutionist may cling to the belief that at some future time he will be able to account for the entrance of LIFE into the world's history, that he will be able to explain the connection of MIND with MATTER; or he may hope that the sterility of certain hybrid forms will one day be explained away, and so on. But till these things *are* got over, the believer cannot be reproached as holding an unreasonable belief when his creed maintains that Life is a gift and prerogative of a great Author of Life; that Mind is the result of a spiritual environment which is a true, though physically intangible, part of nature; and that the absence of any proof that variation and development cross certain - perhaps not very clearly ascertained, but indubitably existing - lines, points to the designed fixing of certain types, and the restriction of developmental creation to running in certain lines of causation up to those types, and not otherwise.

It can never be unreasonable to believe anything that is in exact accordance with facts as ascertained at any given moment of time - unless, indeed, the fact is indicated by other considerations as being one likely to disappear from the category of fact altogether.[1]

Enough has thus, I hope, appeared, to make the appearance of this little work, at least excusable; what more may be necessary to establish its claim to be read must depend on what it contains.

I have only to add that I can make no pretension to be a teacher of science. I trust that there is no material error of statement; if there is, I shall be the first to retract and correct it. I am quite confident that no correction that may be needed in detail will seriously affect the general argument.

CHAPTER II.

THE ELEMENT OF FAITH IN CREATION.

In the extract placed on the title-page, the author of the Epistle clearly places our conclusion that God "established the order of creation" - the lines, plans, developmental-sequences, aims, and objects, that the course of creation has hitherto pursued and is still ceaselessly pursuing,[1] in the category of *faith*.

Of course, from one point of view - very probably that of the writer of the Epistle - this conclusion is argued by the consideration that the human mind forms no distinct conception of the formation of solid - or any other form of - matter *in vacuo*, where nothing previously existed. And what the mind does not find within its own power, but what yet *is true* in the larger spiritual kingdom beyond itself, is apprehended by the spiritual faculty of *faith*.

But from another point of view, the immediate action of faith is not so evident. If, it might be said, the law of evolution, or the law of creation, or whatever is the true law, is, in all its bearings, a matter to be observed and discovered by human science, then it is not easy to see how there is any exercise of faith. We should be more properly said to *know*, by intellectual processes of observation, inference, and conclusion, that there was a Law Giver, an Artificer, and a First Cause, so unlimited in power and capacity by the conditions of the case, that we must call Him "Divine."

And many will probably feel that their just reasoning on the subject leads them to knowledge - knowledge, i.e., as approximately certain as anything in this world can be.

But the text, by the use of the term [Greek: aion], implies (as I suggested) more than mere production of objects; it implies a designed guidance and preconceived planning. If it were merely asserted that there is a first cause of material existence, and even that such a cause had enough known (or to be inferred) about it, to warrant our writing "First Cause" with capitals, then the proposition would pass on all hands without serious question. But directly we are brought face to face, not merely with the isolated idea of creation of tangible forms out of nothing (as the phrase is), but rather with the whole history and development of the world and its inhabitants, we see so many conflicting elements, such a power of natural forces and human passions warring against the progress of good, and seeming to end only too often in disaster, that it becomes a matter of *faith* to perceive a Divine providence underlying and overruling all to its own ends.

The fact is, that directly we make mention of the "aeons" - the world's age histories - we are met with that Protean problem that always seems to lurk at the bottom of every religious question: Why was *evil* permitted? Mr. J.S. Mill, many readers will recollect, concluded that if there was a God, that God was not perfectly good, or else was not omnipotent. Now of course our limited faculties do not enable us to apprehend a really absolute and unlimited omnipotence. We *can* only conceive of God as limited by the terms of His own Nature and Being. We say it is "impossible for God to lie," or for the Almighty to do wrong in any shape; in other words, we are, in this as in other matters where the finite and the Infinite are brought into contact, led up to two necessary conclusions which cannot be reconciled. We can reason out logically and to a full conclusion, that given a God, that God must be perfect, unlimited and unconditioned. We can also reason out, *provided we take purely human and finite premises*, another line of thought which forbids us to suppose that a Perfect God would have allowed evil, suffering, or pain; and this leads us exactly or nearly to Mr. Mill's conclusion.

Whenever we are thus brought up to a dead-lock, as it were, there is the need of *faith*, which is the faculty whereby the finite is linked on to the Infinite. For this faith has two great features: one is represented by the capacity for assimilating fact which is spiritual or transcendental, and therefore not within the reach of finite intellect; the other is represented by the capacity for reliance on, and trust in, the God whose infinite perfections we cannot as finite creatures grasp or follow.

In the difficult scheme of the world's governance, in the storms, earthquakes, pestilences, sufferings of all kinds - signs of failure, sickness, and decay, and death, signs of the victory of evil and the failure of good - we can only *believe* in God, and that all will issue in righteous ends. And our belief proceeds, as just stated, on two lines: one being our spiritual capacity for knowing that GOD IS, and that we, His creatures, are the objects of His love; the other being the fact that we only see a very little end of the thread, or perhaps only a little of one thread out of a vast mass of complicated threads, in the great web of design and governance, and that therefore there is wide ground for confidence that the end will be success. We rely confidently on God. If it is asked, Why is it a part of faith to have a childlike confidence in an unseen God? - we reply, that the main origin of such confidence is to be found in the wonderful condescension of God exhibited in the Incarnation, the Cross, and the Resurrection.

This is not the place to enter on a detailed examination of the essential importance of these great central facts of Christian belief in establishing faith in the unseen, and distinguishing its grasp from the blind clutches of credulity; but a single consideration will suffice at least to awaken a feeling of a wide *vista* of possibility when we put it thus: Do we wonder at the spectacle of a righteous man, passing his life in suffering and poverty, seemingly stricken by the Divine hand? - But is not the case altered when we reflect *that the Hand that thus smites is a hand itself pierced* with the Cross-nails of a terrible human suffering, undergone solely on man's account?

It can be proved easily, by exhaustive examples, to be the case, that wherever the finite is brought into contact with the Infinite, that there must be a dead-lock, a leading up successively to two conclusions, one of which is almost, if not quite, contrary to the other. A very striking instance of this is the question of Predestination and Free-will. From the finite side, I am conscious that I am a free agent: I can will to rise up and to lie down. It is true that my will may be influenced, strongly or feebly, by various means - by the effect of habit, by the inherited tendency of my constitution, by some present motive of temptation, and so forth: but the *will* is there - the motive-influence or inclining-power is not the will, but that which affects or works on will. A *motive* pulls me this way, another pulls me that; but in the end, my *will* follows one or the other. I can, then, do as I please. On the other hand, Infinite Knowledge must know, and have known from all eternity, what I shall do now, and at every moment of my future being: and for Omnipotence to know from all eternity what will be, is, in our human sense, practically undistinguishable from the thought that the Power has predestined the same; and man cannot of course alter that. Here, then, by separate lines of thought, we are brought to two opposite and irreconcilable conclusions. It is so always. We cannot ourselves imagine how a fixed set of laws and rules can be followed, and yet the best interests of each and every one of God's creatures be served as truly as if God directly wielded the machinery of nature only for the special benefit of the individual. The thing is unthinkable to us: yet directly we reason on the necessarily *unlimited* capability of a Divine Providence, we are led to the conclusion that it must be possible. Here then is the province of *Faith*.[1]

It is by Faith, then - combined with only a limited degree of knowledge, founded on observation and reasoning - that we understand that "the aeons were constituted by the Word of God, so that the things which are seen were not made of things which do appear" (the phenomenal has its origin in the non-phenomenal).

While allowing, then, the element of Faith in our recognition of a Creator and Moral Governor of the world, our care is in this, as in all exercises of faith, that our faith be reasonable. We are not called on to believe so as to be "put to confusion," intellectually, as Tait and Balfour have it.

CHAPTER III.

THE DOCTRINE OF CREATION STATED.

It will strike some readers with a sense of hopelessness, this demand for a reason in our faith. A special and very extensive knowledge is required, it seems, to test the very positive assertion that some have chosen to make regarding the "explosion" of the Christian faith in the matter of Creation.

We are told in effect that every thing goes by itself - that given some first cause, about which we know, and can know, nothing, directly primordial matter appears on the scene, and the laws of sequence and action which observed experience has formulated and is progressively formulating are given, then nothing else is required; no governance, no control, and no special design. So that in principle a Creator and Providence are baseless fancies; and this is further borne out by the fact, that when the Christian faith ventures on details as to the mode of Creation it is certainly and demonstrably wrong. If these propositions are to be controverted, it must be in the light of a knowledge which a large body of candid and earnest believers do not possess.

Fortunately, however, the labours of many competent to judge have placed within the reach of the unscientific but careful student, the means of knowing what the conclusions of Science really are, as far as they affect the questions we have to consider. At least, any inquirer can, with a little care and patient study, put himself in a position to know where the difficulty or difficulties lie, and what means there are of getting over them. His want of technical knowledge will not be in his way, so far as his just appreciation of the position is concerned. Without pretending to take up ground which has already been occupied by capable writers whose books can easily be consulted, I may usefully recapitulate in a simple form, and grouped in a suitable order, some of the points best worth noting.

The theory of cosmical evolution is not, in its general idea, a new thing. The sort of evolution, however, that was obscurely shadowed forth by the early sages of India (much as it is the fashion now to allude to it) really stands in no practical relation to the modern and natural theory which is associated with the name of CHARLES DARWIN, and which has been further taken up by Mr. HERBERT SPENCER and others as the foundation for a complete scheme of cosmic philosophy. The theory is now, in its main features, admitted by every one. But there are a few who would push it beyond its real ascertained limits, and would substitute fancies for facts; they are not content to leave the *lacunae*, which undoubtedly do exist, but fill them up by hypothesis,[1] passing by easy steps of forgetfulness from the "it was possibly," "it was likely to have been," to the "it must have been," and "it was"!

To all such extensions we must of course object; there are gaps in the scheme which can be filled in with really great probability, and in such cases there will be no harm done in admitting the probability, while still acknowledging it as such. An overcautious lawyer-like captiousness of spirit in such matters will help no cause and serve no good purpose. Nor is it at all difficult in practice to draw the line and say what is fairly admissible conjecture and what is not. There are other gaps, however, that at present, no real analogy, no fair inferential process, can bridge over; and to all speculations on such subjects, if advanced as more than bare and undisguised guesses, objection must be taken.

If this one line had been fairly and firmly adhered to from the first, it can hardly be doubted that much of the acrimony of controversy would have been avoided. It is just as essential at the present moment to insist on the point as ever. But to proceed. Stated in the extreme form, the theory is, that given matter as a beginning, that matter is thenceforth capable, by the aid of fixed and self-working laws, to produce and result in, all the phenomena of life - whether plant, animal, or human - which we see around us. Matter develops from simple to complex forms, growing by its own properties, in directions determined by the circumstances and surroundings of its existence.

If I may put this a little less in the abstract, but more at length, I should describe it thus[1]: -

Astronomers, while watching the course of the stars, have frequently observed in the heavens what they call *nebulae*. With the best telescopes these look like patches of gold-dust or luminous haze in the sky. Some nebulae, it is supposed, really consist of whole systems of stars and suns, but at so enormous a distance that with our best glasses we cannot make more out of them than groups of apparent "star-dust" But other nebulae do not appear to be at this extreme distance, and therefore cannot consist of large bodies. And when their light is examined with the aid of a spectroscope, it gives indications that such nebulae are only masses of vapour, incandescent, or giving out light on account of their being in a burning or highly heated condition.

Now, it is supposed that, in the beginning of the world, there was, in space, such a nebula or mass of incandescent vapour, which, as it was destined to cool down and form a world, philosophers have called "cosmic gas."

This cosmic gas, in the course of time, began to lose its heat, and consequently to liquefy and solidify, according to the different nature of its components; and thus a globe with a solid crust was formed, the surface of which was partly dry and partly occupied by water, and diversified by the abundant production of the various earths, gases, metals, and other substances with which we are familiar. These substances, in time, and by the slow action of their own laws and properties, combined or separated and produced further forms. But to come at once to the important part of the theory, we must at once direct our attention to four substances; these would certainly, it is said (and that no doubt is quite true) be present; they are oxygen, hydrogen, nitrogen, and carbon. The first three would be, when the earth assumed anything like its present conditions of temperature and air-pressure, invisible gases, as they are at present; the fourth is a substance which forms the basis of charcoal, and which we see in a nearly pure form crystallized in the diamond.

Now, if these substances are brought together under certain appropriate conditions, the oxygen and hydrogen can combine to form *water*; the carbon and the oxygen will form *carbonic acid*; while nitrogen will join with hydrogen to form that pungent smelling substance with which we are familiar as *ammonia*. Again, let us suppose that three compound substances - water, carbonic acid, and ammonia - are present together with appropriate conditions; it is said that they will combine to form a gummy transparent matter, which is called *protoplasm*. This protoplasm may be found in small shapeless lumps, or it may be found enclosed in cells, and in various beautifully shaped coverings, and it is also found in the blood, and in all growing parts or organs of all animals and plants of every kind whatsoever.

Protoplasm, then, is the physical basis of life. Simple, uniform, shapeless protoplasm, combined out of the substances just named, first came into existence; and as, however simple or shapeless, it always exhibits the property of life, it can henceforth grow and develop from simpler to ever increasingly complex forms, without any help but that of surrounding circumstances - the secondary causes which we see in operation around us.

If some readers should say they have never seen *protoplasm*, I may remind them where every one has, at some time or another, met with it. If you cut a stick of new wood from a hedge, and peel off the young bark, you know that the bark comes off easily and entire, leaving a clean white wand of wood in your hand; but the wand feels sticky all over. This sticky stuff is nothing more than transparent growing protoplasm, which lies close under the inner bark.

At first, the materialist holds, protoplasm appeared in

very simple forms, just such as can still be found within the sea, and in ponds. But the lower organized forms of life are extremely unstable, and a different *environment* will always tend to evoke continuous small changes, so that there may be advance in forms of all kinds. For if by chance[1] some creature exhibits a variation which is favourable to it in the circumstances in which it is placed, that creature will be fitter than the others which have not that variation. And so the former will survive, and as they multiply, their descendants will inherit the peculiarity. Thus, in the course of countless generations, change will succeed change, till creatures of quite a complex structure and specialized form have arisen. As the circumstances of life are always infinitely various, the developments take place in many different directions; some fit the creature for life in deep seas, some for flying in the air, some for living in holes and crevices, some for catching prey by swift pursuit, others for catching it by artful contrivance, and so forth. Many changes will also arise from protective necessity: if an insect happens to be like a dead leaf, it will escape the notice of birds which would snap up a conspicuously coloured one; and so the dull-coloured will survive and perpetuate his kind, while the others are destroyed. On the other hand, beauty in colour and form may have its use. This is chiefly exhibited in the preference which the females of a species show for the adorned and showy males.

Supposing an organism developed so far as to be a bird, but only with dull or ugly feathers. By accident one male bird, say, gets a few bright-coloured feathers on his head. Here his appearance will attract birds of the other sex; and then by the law of heredity, his offspring are sure to repeat the coloured feathers, till at last a regularly bright-crested species-arises. In this way *natural variability*, acted on by the necessities of *environment* (which cause the *survival of the fittest* specimens) and the principle of *heredity*, viz., that the offspring repeat the features of the parents, aided by the principle of *sexual selection*, have been the origin and cause of all the species we see in the world.

Thus we have an unbroken series - certain substances condensing out of cosmic vapour, some of them combining to form the variety of rocks, soils, metals, &c., and others giving rise to protoplasm which grows' and develops into a thousand shapes and hues, of insect, fish, reptile, bird, and beast.

And then it is, that charmed with the completeness and symmetry of such a theory, and overlooking the difficulties that crop up here and here - demanding some Power from without to bridge them over - certain extreme theorists have rushed to the conclusion that in all this there is no need of any external Creator or Providence - nothing but what we call secondary causes, ordinary causes which we see at work around us all day and every day.

How inconceivable, they add, is the truth of the Book of Genesis, which asserts the successive creation of fully-formed animals by sudden acts of command; and all accomplished in a few days at the beginning of the world's human history!

This I believe to be a fair outline, though of course a very rough and general one, of the Theory of Evolution as regards the forms of matter and living organisms. Now it will at once strike the candid reader, that even granted the whole of the scheme as stated, there is *nothing* in it that has any answer to the objection, - But may I not believe that a wise Creator conceived and established the whole plan - first creating MATTER and FORCE, then superadding LIFE at a certain stage, and then drawing out the type and design according to which everything was to grow and develop? Is not such a production and such a design the true essence of Creation? Can all these things happen *without* such aid? Let us then look more closely at some of the steps in the evolution just described. And let us stop at the very beginning - the first term of the series.

We may agree (in the absence of anything leading to a contrary conclusion) that matter may first have appeared as a cosmic gas, or incandescent vapour in space. It is probable, if not certain, that our earth is a mass that has only cooled down on the surface, the centre being still hot and to some extent, at any rate, molten; and in the sun we have the case of an enormous globe surrounded with a *photosphere*, as it is called - a blaze of incandescent substances, which our spectroscopes tell us are substances such as we have on earth now in cooled or condensed condition - iron, oxygen, hydrogen, and other such forms of matter.

First of all, how did any *substance*, however vapoury and tenuous, come to exist, when previously there was nothing?

If we admit, that there was a time when even cosmic gas did not exist, then there must have been *an Agent*, whose *fiat* caused the change. And as that Agent does not obviously belong to the material order, it must belong to the spiritual or non-material; for the two orders together exhaust the possibilities of existence. If, however, it is urged that "primal matter" - cosmic vapour - containing the "potentiality" of all existence, is eternal and alway existed of itself, then we are brought face to face with innumerable difficulties. In the first place, the existence of matter is not the only difficulty to be got over; not the only dead-lock along the line. We pass it over and go on for a time, and then we come to another - the introduction of LIFE. I will not pause to consider that here; we shall see presently that it is impossible to regard life as merely a quality or property of matter. When we have passed that, we have a third stoppage, the introduction of *Reason* or *Intelligence*; and then a fourth, the introduction of the *Spiritual faculties*, which cannot be placed on the same footing as mere reason. So that to get over the first point, and dispense with a Cause or a Creator of matter, is of no avail: it is incredible that there should be no Creator of matter, but that there should be a Creator of life - an Imparter of reason, an Endower of soul.

But let us revert to the first stage and look at the nature of MATTER.

CHAPTER IV.

CREATIVE DESIGN IN INORGANIC MATTER.

I take as self-evident the enormous difficulty of self-caused, self-existent matter. And when we see that matter *acting*, not irregularly or by caprice, but *by law* (as every class of philosopher will admit), then it is still further difficult to realize that matter not only existed as a dead, simple, inactive thing, but existed with a folded-up history inside it, a long sequence of development - not the same for all particles, but various for each group: so that one set proceeded to form the *object*, and another the *environment* of the object; or rather that a multitude of sets formed a vast variety of objects, and another multitude of sets formed a vast variety of environments. When we see matter acting by law, then if there is no Creator, we have the to us unthinkable proposition of law without a lawgiver!

On the other hand, if we shut out some of the difficulties, keep our eye on one part of the case only - and that is what the human mind is very apt to do - we can easily come round to think that, after all, *elementary* matter - cosmic gas - is a very *simple* thing; and looks really as if no great Power, or Intellect, were required to account for its origin. After all, some will say, if we grant your great, wise, beneficent, designing

Creator, the finite human mind has as little idea of a self-existing God, as it has of self-existing matter and self-existing law. *You* postulate one great mystery, *we* postulate two smaller ones; and the two together really present less "unthinkableness" to the mind than your one. That is so far plausible, but it is no more. To believe in a GOD is to believe in One Existence, who necessarily (by the terms of our conception) has the power both of creating matter, designing the forms it shall take, and originating the tendencies, forces, activities - or whatever else we please to call them - which drive matter in the right direction to get the desired result. To believe not only that matter caused itself, but that the different forces and tendencies, and the aims and ends of development, were self-caused, is surely a much more difficult task. It is the existence of such a *variety*, it is the existence of a uniform tendency to produce certain though multitudinous results, that makes the insuperable difficulty of supposing *matter always developing* (towards certain ends) to be self-caused.

The advocates of "eternal matter" really overcome the difficulty, by shutting their eyes to everything beyond a part of the problem - the existence of simple matter apart from any laws, properties, or affinities.

But the simplest drop of water, in itself, and apart from its mechanical relations to other matter, is really a very complex and a very wonderful thing; not at all likely to be "self-caused." Water is made up, we know, of oxygen and hydrogen - two elementary colourless, formless gases. Now we can easily divide the one drop into two, and, without any great difficulty, the two into four, and (perhaps with the aid of a magnifying glass) the four into eight, and so on, *as long as* the minute particle *still retains the nature of water*. In short, we speak of the smallest subdivision of which matter is capable without losing its own nature, as the *molecule*. All matter may be regarded as consisting of a vast mass of these small molecules.

Now, we know that all known matter is capable of existing either in a solid, liquid, or gaseous form, its nature not being changed. Water is very easily so dealt with. Some substances, it is true, require very great pressure or very great cold, or both, to alter their form; but even carbonic acid, oxygen, and hydrogen, which under ordinary conditions are gases, can with proper appliances be made both liquid and solid. Pure alcohol, has, I believe, never been made solid, but that is only because it is so difficult to get a sufficient degree of cold: there is no doubt that it could be done.

It might be supposed that the molecules of which dead matter (whether solid, liquid, or vapourous) is composed, were equally motionless and structureless. But it is not so: every molecule in its own kind is endowed with marvellous properties. In the first place, every molecule has a double capability of motion. In the solid form the molecules are so packed together that, of course, the motion is excessively restricted; in the liquid it is a little easier; in the gaseous state the molecules are in a comparatively "open order." In most substances that are solid under ordinary conditions, by applying heat continuously we first liquefy and ultimately vapourize them. In those substances which under ordinary conditions are *gas* (like carbonic acid, for instance), it is by applying cold, with perhaps great pressure as well, that we induce them to become liquid and solid; in fact, the process is just reversed. As we can most easily follow the process of heating, I will describe that. First, the solid (in most cases) gets larger and larger as it progresses to liquefaction, and when it gets to vapour, it suddenly expands enormously. Take a rod of soft iron, and reduce it to freezing temperature: let us suppose that in that condition it measures just a thousand inches long. Then raise the temperature to 212 degrees (boiling point), and it will be found to measure 1,012 inches. Why is that? Obviously, because the molecules have got a little further apart. If you heat it till the iron gets liquid, the liquid would also occupy still more space than the original solid rod; and if we had temperature high enough to make the melted iron go off into vapour, it would occupy an enormously increased space. I cannot say what it would be for iron vapour; but if a given volume of water is converted into vapour, it will occupy about 1,700 times the space it did when liquid, though the weight would not be altered.

It may here be worth while to mention that it is not invariably true that a substance gets contracted, and the molecules more and more pressed together, as it assumes a solid form. There is at least one exception. If we take 1,700 pints of steam, the water, as I said, on becoming cool enough to lose the vapourous form, will shrink into a measure holding a single pint; if we cooled lower still, it will get smaller and smaller in bulk (though of course not at all at the same rate) till it arrives at a point when it is just going to freeze; then suddenly (7 degrees above the freezing point) it again begins to expand. Ice occupies more space than cold water; its molecules get arranged in a particular manner by their crystallization.

On the admission of an *intelligent* Creator providing, by beneficent design, the laws of matter, it is easy to give a reason for this useful property. It prevents the inhabitants of northern climates being deprived of a supply of water. As it is, the solid water or ice expands, and, becoming lighter, forms at the top of the water, and the heavier warmer water remains below. But if ice always got denser and sank, the warmer liquid would be perpetually displaced and so come up to the surface, where it would freeze and sink in its turn. In a short time, then, all our water supplies would (whenever the temperature went down to freezing, which it constantly does in winter) be turned into solid ice. This would be a source of the gravest inconvenience to the population of a cold climate. If we deny a designing mind, the alternative is that this property of water is a mere chance.

But to return to molecules. Molecules are endowed with an inherent faculty of motion; only under the conditions of what we call the solid, they are so compressed, that there is no room for any motion appreciable to the senses. Even if the solid is converted into vapour, the molecules are still much restrained in their movements by the pressure of the air. But of late years, great improvements (partly chemical, partly mechanical) have been made in producing perfect *vacua*; that is to say, in getting glass or other vessels to be so far empty of air, that the almost inconceivably small residue in the receptacle has no perceptible effect on the action of a small quantity of any substance already reduced to the form of gas or vapour introduced into it. Dr. W. Crookes has made many beautiful experiments on the behaviour of the molecules of attenuated matter in *vacua*. The small quantity of vapour introduced contains only a relatively small number of molecules, which thus freed from all sensible restraint within the limits of the glass vessel used, are free to move as they will; they are observed to rush about, to strike against the sides of the vessel, and under proper conditions to shine and become *radiant*, and to exhibit extraordinary phenomena when subjected to currents of electricity. So peculiar is the molecular action thus set up, that scientific men have been tempted to speak of a fourth condition of matter (besides the three ordinary ones, solid, liquid, and gaseous), which they call the ultra-gaseous or radiant state of matter.

This marvel of molecular structure seems already to have removed us sufficiently far from the idea of a simple inert mass, which might be primordial and self-caused. But we have not yet done. Even imagining the extreme subdivision[1] of the particles in one of Dr. Crookes' vacuum globes, the particles are still water. But we know that water is a compound substance. The molecule has nine parts, of which eight are hydrogen and one oxygen - because that is the experimentally known proportion in which oxygen and hydrogen combine to form water. As we can (in the present state of our knowledge) divide no farther, we call these ultimate fragments of simple or elementary substance *atoms*.

Every substance, however finely divided into molecules, if it is not a simple substance, must therefore have, inside the *molecular* structure, a further *atomic* structure. And in the case of unresolvable or "elementary" substance, the molecule and the atom are not necessarily the same. For though there is reason to believe that, the molecule of these does consist, in some cases, of only one atom - in which case the atom and the molecule are identical; in other cases, the molecule is known to consist of more than one atom of the same element; and the atoms are capable of being differently arranged, and when so arranged have different *properties* or behaviour, though their nature is not changed. This property is spoken of by chemists as *allotropism*. No chemist on earth can detect the slightest difference in *constitution* between a molecule of *ozone* and one *oxygen*; but the two have widely different properties, or behave very differently. There is thus a great mystery about atoms and their possible differences under different arrangement, which is as yet unsolved. Those who wish to get an insight into the matter (which cannot be pursued farther here) will do well to read Josiah Cooke's "The New Chemistry," in the International Scientific Series. The mind is really lost in trying to realize the idea of a fragment of matter too small for the most powerful microscope, but existing in fact (because of faultless reasoning from absolutely conclusive experiments), and yet so constituted that it is *practically* a different thing when placed in one position or order, from what it is when placed in another.

Turning from this mystery, as yet so obscure, to what is more easily grasped, we shall hardly be surprised to learn, further, that every kind of, atom obeys its own laws, and that while atoms of one kind always have a *tendency to combine* with atoms of other kinds, it is absolutely impossible to get them to combine together except on certain conditions.

The difference between combination and mixture is well known. Shake sand and sugar in a bag for ever so long, but they will only *mix*, not *combine* or form any new substance even with the aid of electric currents; but place oxygen and hydrogen gas under proper conditions, and the gases will disappear, and water (in weight exactly equal to the weight of the volume of gases) will appear in their place.

It is only certain kinds of atoms that will combine at all with other kinds; and when they do so combine, they will only unite in absolutely fixed proportions, so that chemists have been able to assign to every kind of element its own combining proportion. The substances that will combine will do so in these proportions, or in proportions of any *even multiple* of the number, and in no other. Thus fourteen parts of nitrogen will combine with sixteen of oxygen; and we have several substances in nature, called nitrous oxide, nitric oxide, nitric di-oxide, &c., which illustrate this, in which fourteen parts of nitrogen combine with sixteen oxygen or fourteen nitrogen with a multiple of sixteen oxygen, or a multiple of fourteen nitrogen combine with sixteen oxygen, and so on.

See now where we have got to. When we had spoken of a tiny fragment of primal matter - a drop of water, for instance - it seemed as if there was no more to be said; but no, we found ourselves able to give a whole history of the molecules of which the substance consists; and when we had considered the molecule, we found a further beautiful and intricate order of *atoms* inside the molecule, as it were.

And there is no reason to suppose that science has yet revealed all that is possible to be known about atoms and molecules; so that if further wonders should be evoked, the argument will grow and grow in cumulative force.

Let me sum up the conclusion to be drawn from these facts in a quotation from a discourse of Sir

John F.W. Herschel.

"When we see," says that eminent philosopher, "a great number of things precisely alike, we do not believe this similarity to have originated except from *a common principle independent of them*; and that we recognize this likeness, chiefly by the *identity of their deportment under similar circumstances* strengthens rather than weakens the conclusion.

"A line of spinning jennies, or a regiment of soldiers dressed exactly alike and going through precisely the same evolutions, gives us no idea of independent existence: we must see them act out of concert before we can believe them to have independent wills and properties not impressed on them from without.

"And this conclusion, which would be strong even if there were only two individuals precisely alike in *all* respects and *for ever*, acquires irresistible force when their number is multiplied beyond the power of imagination to conceive.

"If we mistake not, then, the discoveries alluded to effectually destroy the ideas of an *eternal* self-existent matter by giving to each of its atoms the essential characters at once of a *manufactured* article and of a *subordinate agent*."

In other words, continuing the metaphor of the trained army, we see millions upon millions of molecules all arranged in regiments, distinct and separate, and the regiments again made up of companies or individuals, each obeying his own orders in subordination to, and in harmony with, the whole: are we not justified in concluding that this army has not been only called into being by some cause external to itself; but further, that its constitution has been impressed upon it, and its equipments and organization directed, by an Infinite Intelligence?

There is, then, no such thing to be found in Nature as a simple, structureless "primal matter" which exhibits nothing tending to make self-causation or aboriginal existence difficult to conceive. To look at matter in that light is not only to take into consideration a *part* of the case; it is really to take what does not exist, a part that exists only in the imagination. The simplest form of matter we can deal with, exhibits within itself all the wondrous plan, law, and sequence of the molecular and atomic structure we have sketched out; and when we consider that, having taken matter so far, we have even then only introduced it to the verge of the universe, ushered it on to the threshold of a great "aeon," when and where it is to be acted on by "gravitation" and other forces, to act in relation to other matter, and to be endowed perhaps with LIFE, we shall feel that the self-existence - the uncaused existence of matter, and of the principles on which matter proceeds or acts, is in reality not a less mystery than the self-existence of a Designing and Intelligent Cause, but one so great as to be itself "unthinkable."

CHAPTER V.

THE CREATION OF LIVING MATTER.

We now come to *Living* Matter; directing attention, first, to that elementary form of life as exhibited in simple protoplasm and in the lower forms of organism, and then to the perfect forms of bird and beast. In each case, we shall find the same evidence of Design and Intelligence, the same proof of "contrivance" and purpose, which we cannot attribute to the mere action of secondary causes.

The simplest form in which LIFE is manifested is in a viscid gelatinous substance without colour or form, called *Protoplasm*. Wherever there is life there is protoplasm. Protoplasm, as before remarked, lies just under the bark in trees, and is the material from which the growth of the wood and bark cells and fibres proceeds. Protoplasm, is also present in the muscles and in the blood, and wherever growth is going on.

But protoplasm also exists by itself; or, more properly speaking, there exist living creatures, both plant and animal, which are so simple in structure, so low in organization, that they consist of nothing but a speck of protoplasm. Such a creature is the microscopic *amoeba*. Sometimes these little specks of protoplasm are surrounded with beautifully formed "silicious shells - a skeleton of radiating *spiculae* or crystal-clear concentric spheres of exquisite symmetry and beauty.[1]" The simplest *amoeba* however, has no definite form; but the little mass moves about, expands and contracts, throws out projections on one side and draws them in on the other. It exhibits irritability when touched. It may be seen surrounding a tiny particle of food, extracting nutriment from it and growing in size. Ultimately the little body separates or splits up into two, each part thenceforth taking a separate existence.

Now it is claimed that such a little organism contains the potentiality of all life; that it grows and multiplies, and develops into higher and higher organisms, into all (in short) that we see in the plant and animal world around us. This, it is argued, is all done by natural causes, not by any direction or guidance or intervention of a Divine agency.

Here we must stop to ask how this protoplasm, or simplest form of organic life, came to exist? How did it get its *life* - its property of taking nourishment, of growing and of giving birth to other creatures like itself?

The denier of creation replies, that just in the same way as, by the laws of affinity, other inanimate substances came together to produce the earth - salts and other compounds we see in the world around us - so did certain elements combine to form protoplasm. This combination when perfected has the property of being alive, just as water has the property of assuming a solid form or has any other of the qualities which we speak of as its properties.

Now it is perfectly true that, treated as a substance, you

can take the gummy protoplasm, put it into a glass and subject it to analysis like any other substance. But simple as the substance appears, composition is really very complicated. Professor Allman tells us that so difficult and wonderful is its chemistry, that in fact really very little is known about it. The best evidence we have, I believe, makes it tolerably certain that protoplasm consists of a combination of ammonia, carbonic acid, and water, and that every molecule of it is made up of 76 atoms, of which 36 are carbon, 26 hydrogen, 4 nitrogen, and 10 oxygen.[1]

But no chemist has ever been able either to account theoretically for such a composition, still less to produce it artificially. It is urged, however, that it may be only due to our clumsy apparatus and still very imperfect knowledge of chemistry, that we were unable artificially to make up protoplasm.

And of course there is no answer to a supposition of this sort. Nevertheless there is no sort of reason to believe that protoplasm will ever be made; nor, if we could succeed in uniting the elements into a form resembling protoplasmic jelly, is there the least reason to suppose that such a composition would exhibit the irritability, or the powers of nutrition and reproduction, which are essentially the characteristics of *living* protoplasm. It is not too much to say that, after the close of the controversy about spontaneous generation, it is now a universally admitted principle of science that life can only proceed from life - the old *omne vivum ex ovo* in a modern form.[1]

But here the same sort of argument that was brought forward regarding the possibility of matter and its laws being self-caused, comes in as regards life.

The argument in the most direct form was made use of by Professor Huxley, but it is difficult to believe that so powerful a thinker could seriously hold to a view which will not bear examination, however neatly and brilliantly it may go off when first launched into the air. The argument is that life can only be regarded as a further property of certain forms of matter. Oxygen and hydrogen, when they combine, result in a new substance, quite unlike either of them in character, and possessing *new* and different properties. The way in which the combination is effected is a mystery, yet we do not account for the new and peculiar properties of water (so different from those of the original gases) as arising from a principle of "aquosity," which we have to invoke from another world. The answer is that the argument is from analogy, and that there is not really the remotest analogy between the two cases. It is true that, as far as we know, electricity is necessary to force a combination of the requisite equivalents of oxygen and hydrogen into water. But though we do not know why this is, or what electricity is, we can repeat the process as often as we will. But mark the difference; the water once existing is obviously only a new form of matter, in the same category with the gases it came from: it neither increases in bulk, nor takes in fresh elements to grow, and give birth to new drops of water. But protoplasm has something quite different - for there may be dead protoplasm and living protoplasm, both identical to the eye and to every chemical test. In either condition, protoplasm, as such, has *properties* of the same nature (though not of the same kind) as those of water, oxygen gas, or any other matter; it is colorless, heavy, sticky, elastic, and so forth; but besides all that (without the aid of electricity or any physical force we can apply) one has the power of producing more protoplasm - gathering for itself, by virtue of its inherent power, the materials for growth and reproduction.

If directly water was called into existence it could take in nourishment, and divide and go on producing more water - and if some water could do this, while other water (which no available test could distinguish from it in any other respect) could not, then we *should* be perfectly justified in giving a special name to this power, and calling it "aquosity" or "vitality" or anything else, it being out of all analogy to anything else which we call a "property" of matter.

In the introduction of LIFE into the *aeon* of organic developmental history, we have a clear and distinct period, as we had when *matter* came into view, or when *the change* was ushered in which set the cosmic gas cooling and liquefying, and turning to solid in various form.

The fact is that every organic form, whether plant or animal, derived from the protoplasmic compounds of carbon-dixoide, ammonia and water, is, as Mr. Drummond puts it,[1] "made of materials which have once been inorganic. An organizing principle, not belonging to their kingdom, lays hold of them and elaborates them."

Thus by the introduction of LIFE we have a vastly enlarged horizon. Before, in the organic world, we had only the "principle" of solidifying or crystallizing, liquefying, and turning to gas or vapour, ever stopping when the state was attained. Or if a combination was in progress, still the result was only a rearrangement of the same bulk of materials (however new the form) in solid, liquid, or gas, but no increase, no nutrition, no reproduction. In the organic world we have something so different, that whether we talk of "property" or "principle," the things are entirely distinct.

The essential difference, stated as regards the mere facts of irritability or motion, nutrition and reproduction, is so grandly sufficient in itself, that one almost regrets to have to add on the other facts which further emphasize the distinction between *life* and any *property* of matter. But these further facts are highly important as regards another part of the argument. For while what has just been said almost demonstrates the necessity of a Giver of Life from a kingdom outside the organic, the further facts point irresistibly to the conclusion that we must predicate more about the Giver of Life that we can of an abstract and unknown Cause.

The original protoplasm, when dead, is undistinguishable by the eye, by chemical test, or by the microscope, from the same protoplasm when living; and living protoplasm, again, may be either animal or vegetable. Both are in every respect (externally) absolutely identical. Yet the one will only develop into a *plant*, the other only into an *animal*. Nor does it diminish the significance of the fact to say that the differentiation is *now* fixed by heredity. If we suppose protoplasm to be only a fortuitous combination of elements, what secondary or common natural cause will account for its acquisition of the fixed difference? It is true that some forms of plants exhibit some functions that closely approach the functions of what we call animal life; but, as we shall see presently, there is no evidence whatever that there is any bridge between the two - we have no proof that a plant ever develops into an animal. Here is one of the gaps which the theory of Evolution, true as it is to a certain extent, cannot bridge over; and we must not overlook the fact. We shall revert to it hereafter.

Can it be believed, then, that protoplasm, as the origin of life, is self-caused, and self-developed? And this is not all. I must briefly remind my readers that the way in which animal protoplasm deals with the elements of nutrition is quite opposite to that which plant protoplasm follows. I might, indeed, have mentioned this at an earlier stage, when I mentioned Professor Huxley's comparison of the chemical action in the formation of water with what he assumed to be the case in the formation of protoplasm. When water is formed, the two gases disappear, and an *exactly equal weight* of water appears in their place; but if living protoplasm is enabled to imbibe liquid or other nutriment containing ammonia, water, and carbonic acid, there is no disappearance of the three elements and an equivalent weight of living protoplasm appearing in its place. Protoplasm consumes the oxygen and sets free the carbonic acid. Both kinds of protoplasm do this, until exposed to the light; and then a difference is observed; for under the influence of light, animal protoplasm alone continues to act in this way, and vegetable protoplasm begins at once to develop little green bodies or corpuscles in its cells, and afterwards acts in a totally opposite way, taking the carbon into its substance and giving off the oxygen.[1]

Not only then has each kind of protoplasm its own mysterious character impressed on it, and is compelled to act in a certain way; but still further, each particle of animal and vegetable protoplasm, when directed into its *general* course of development as *plant or animal*, will again only obey a certain course of development in its own line.

But we must proceed a step further; for those who would believe in the sufficiency of unaided Evolution, bid us bear in mind how very elementary the dawn of instinct or the beginning of reason is in the lowest forms which are classed as animal, and how very small is the gap[1] between some highly organized plants and some animal forms, and argue therefore that they may justly regard the distinction as of minor importance, and hope that the "missing link" will be yet discovered and proved. At any rate, they minimize the difference, and urge that it is of no account if at least they can establish the sufficiency of a proved development extending unbroken from the lowest to the highest animal form. And having fixed attention on this side, no doubt there is a long stretch of smooth water over which the passage is unchecked.

The Evolution theory is that all the different species of animals, birds, and other forms of life have been caused by the accumulation and perpetuation of numerous small changes which began in one or at most a few elementary forms, and went on till all the thousands of species we now know of were developed.[1] It *is* a fact that all organic forms have a certain tendency to vary. I need only allude to the many varieties of pigeons, horses, cattle, and dogs which are produced by varying the food, the circumstances of life and so forth, and by selective breeding.

The contention then is: given certain original simple forms of life, probably marine or aquatic - for it is in the water that the most likely occur - these will gradually change and vary, some in one direction, some in another; that the changes go on increasing, each creature giving birth to offspring which exhibits the stored-up results of change, till the varied and finished forms - some reptile, some bird, some animal - which we now see around us, have been produced. And at last man himself was developed in the same way. All this, observe, is by the action of just such ordinary and natural causes as we now see operating around us - changes in food and in climate, changes in one part requiring a corresponding change in others, and so on.

Nature contains no sharply drawn lines. Plants are different from animals; but there are animals so low down in the scale of life that it is difficult to distinguish them from plants. Pigeons are distinct from pheasants, but the line at which the one species ends and the other begins is difficult to draw. This fact seems to invite some theory of one form changing into other. Accordingly the evolutionist explains the working of the process which he asserts to be sufficient to produce all the various forms of life in our globe.

After stating this more in detail than we have previously done, we shall be in a better position to judge if the process (which in the main we have no desire to deny or even to question) can dispense with *guidance* and the fixing of certain lines and limits within which, and of certain types towards which, the development proceeds. That is our point.

It is hardly necessary to illustrate the enormous destruction of life which goes on in the world. Even among the human race, the percentage of infants that die in the first months of their life is very large. But in the lower forms of life it is truly enormous. Only consider the myriads of insects that perish from hunger or accident, and from the preying of one species on another. If it were not so, the world would be overrun by plagues of mice, of birds, of insects of all kinds, and indeed by creatures of every grade. The term "struggle for existence" is, then, not an inapt one. All forms of living creatures have to contend with enemies which seek to prey upon or to destroy them, with the difficulty of obtaining food, and with what I may call the chances of nature - cold, storms, floods, disease, and so forth.

Now, it is obvious that if some creatures of a given kind possess some accidental peculiarity or modification in their formation which gives them (in one way or another) an advantage over their fellows, these improved specimens are likely to survive, and, surviving, to have offspring.

It is this perpetuation of advantageous changes, originally induced by the circumstances of environment, that is indicated by the term "natural selection." Nature chooses out the form best suited to the circumstances which surround it, and this form lives while the others die out. And this form goes on improving by slow successive changes, which make it more and more fit for the continually changing circumstances of its life.

Subordinate also to this natural selection is the principle that bright colour and other special qualities may be developed in the males of a race, because individuals with such advantages are more attractive, and therefore more easily find mates, than dull-coloured or otherwise less attractive individuals.

Of each of these principles I may give a simple example. Supposing a species of bird with a soft slender beak to be placed on an island, where the only food they could obtain was fruit enclosed in a hard or tough shell or covering. Supposing some birds accidentally possessed of a beak that was shorter and stouter than the others', these would be able to break open the shell and get at the fruit, while the others would starve. Some of the descendants of the birds with the stout beaks would inherit the same peculiarity, and in the course of several generations there would thus arise a species with short and strong, perhaps curved, beaks just fitted to live on fruits of the kind described. In a similar way the webbed feet of birds that swim were developed by their aquatic habits. And so with the long slender toes of the waders, which are so well fitted for walking over floating aquatic plants.

Of the other principle, sexual selection, a familiar example is the bright and showy colouring of the male birds of many species: the females of their species, as they need protection while helplessly sitting on their eggs, are dull-coloured like the bark of trees or the sand, among which their nests lie hid.

Some of the Himalayan pheasants exhibit this peculiarity to a marked degree. Originally, it is said, the male bird, which was more brightly coloured than the rest, got mated more easily by the preference shown to him for his bright colour.

The question is, can we suppose all this to go on, by self-caused laws and concurrence of circumstances, without a pre-existing design for the forms to reach or an external guidance in the processes?

CHAPTER VI.

THE MARKS OF CREATIVE INTELLIGENCE IN THE EVOLUTION OF ORGANIC FORMS.

The heading of this chapter does not mark a new departure, for we have been tracing existing forms of matter from the first, and have already seen the necessity of believing in Creative Intelligence and Guidance. We have seen that inorganic matter, with what we call its molecular or atomic structure, cannot be reasonably regarded as self-caused; and we have concluded with Sir J.F.W. Herschell that the sight of such a well-arranged army, performing its evolutions in a regular and uniform manner, irresistibly suggests a great Commander and Designer. We have further found that the advent of LIFE demands a Power *ab extra*. We have called attention to the gap, between plant and animal, which is ignored or made light of, chiefly on account of the close approach of the two kingdoms. But there is one broad distinction, namely, that of elementary reason and no reason, or of consciousness and unconsciousness, which is, in itself, a sufficient difficulty to pull us up shortly. We have not yet fully considered this matter, because it will come more appropriately at a later stage, and in the *a fortiori* form. But we have justly noted it here. We cannot account for the most elementary reason by any physical change; there is no analogy between the two.

The connection of mind and matter is unexplainable; and no theory of development of physical form can say why, at any given stage, physical development begins to be accompanied by brain-power and *consciousness*. Admit candidly that the addition of intelligence at a certain stage, however mysteriously interwoven with structural accompaniments, is a gift *ab extra*, and we have at least a reasonable and so far satisfactory explanation.

But when we have got an animal form, however simple and elementary, with at least a recognizable "potentiality" of intelligence, we enter, as I said, a long stretch of apparently smooth water, over which, for an important part of our passage, we seem able to glide without any difficulty from the necessary intervention of the so-called supernatural. I have, then, to show that even here there is really no possibility of dispensing with a Creator who has a purpose, a designed scheme, and a series of type-forms to be complied with.

In order to fully exhaust the question how far natural selection is capable of accounting for everything, it would be necessary to take a very wide view of natural history and botany, which it is quite impossible for us to attempt. But this is not necessary for our purpose. We are perfectly justified in selecting certain topics which must arise in the discussion. If, in studying these points, we find that *there* at least the intervention of a Controlling Power becomes necessary, and the absence of it leaves things without any reasonable explanation, then we shall have good and logical ground for holding to our faith in the universal presence of such a Power. No chain is stronger than its weakest link. If secondary causes cannot succeed at any one part of the chain, it is obvious that they fail as a universal explanation.

This part of the work has already been done far better than I could do it. In the first eight chapters of Mivart's "Genesis of Species" [1] the argument has been ably and clearly put, and whatever answer is possible has been given by Darwin and others; so that the world may judge. All that can here be usefully attempted, is, by way of reminder, to reproduce some main topics on which no real answer has been given. These are selected, partly because they are less abstruse and difficult to follow than some which might be dealt with, partly because they are calculated to awaken our interest, and partly because the conclusion in favour of a continual Providence; working through organized law and system, appears to follow most clearly from them.

The points I would call attention to are the following: -

(1) That as natural selection will only maintain changes that have been *beneficial* to the creature, it is contrary to such a law, if acting entirely by itself, that that there should be developments (not being mere accidental deformities, &c.) disadvantageous to the creature. And yet the world is full of such.

(2) That there are forms which cannot be accounted for on the evolutionist supposition, that they were gradually obtained by a series of small changes slowly progressing towards a perfect structure. They would be of no use at all unless produced *at once and complete*.

(3) That natural selection, as apart from a Divine Designer, altogether fails to account for *beauty*, as distinguished from mere brilliancy or conspicuousness, in nature. Whereas, if we suppose the existence of a beneficent Creator, who has moral objects in view, and

cares for the delight and the improvement of His creatures,[1] and looking to the known effects on the mind of beauty in art and in nature, the existence is at once and beyond all cavil explained.

(4) That we have positive evidence against *uncontrolled* evolution (uncontrolled by set plan and design i.e.) and a strong presumption in favour of the existence of created *types*; so that evolution proceeds towards these types by aid of natural laws and forces working together (in a way that our limited faculties necessarily fail to grasp adequately);[1] and so that, the type once reached, a certain degree of variation, but never *transgression* of *the type*, is possible. Further, that on this supposition we are able to account for some of the unexplained facts in evolutionary history, such as *reversion* and the *sterility of hybrids*; and to see why there are gaps which cannot be bridged over, and which by extreme theorists are only feebly accounted for on the supposition that as discovery progresses they *will* be bridged over some day.

(5) Lastly, that there is no possibility of giving *time* enough on any possible theory of the world's existence, for the evolution of all species, unless *some* reasonable theory of creative arrangement and design be admitted.

The great objection - the descent of man and the introduction of reason, consciousness, and so forth, into the world, will then form two separate chapters, concluding the first division of my subject.

There is one point which the reader may be surprised to see omitted. It is, that if these slow changes were always going on, why is not the present world full of, and the fossil-bearing rocks also abounding in, *intermediate forms*, creatures which *are on their way* to being something else? But there are reasons to be given on this ground which make the subject a less definite one for treatment. It is said, for example, that in the fossil rocks we have only such scanty and fragmentary records, that it is not possible to draw a complete inference, and that there is always the possibility of fresh discoveries being made. Such discoveries have, it is asserted, already been made in the miocene and again in later rocks; different species of an early form of *horse* which are (and this we may admit) the ancestral or intermediate forms of our own horse, have been found. I therefore would not press the difficulty, great as it is, because of the escape which the hope of future discovery always affords. I will take this opportunity to repeat that in this chapter I say nothing about the difficulty which arises from the introduction of elementary reason or instinct, and of consciousness, into the scale of organic being; that will more appropriately fall in with the consideration of the development of man, where naturally the difficulty occurs with its greatest force.

(1) I come at once to the great difficulty that, if all existing forms are due to the occurrence of changes that helped the creature in the struggle for existence, how is it possible now to account for forms which are not advantageous? yet such forms are numerous. Of this objection, the existence of imperfect or neuter bees and ants is an instance. The modification in form which these creatures exhibit is of no advantage to them. It *is* a great advantage, no doubt, to the other bees; but then this introduces a view of some power *making* one thing for the benefit of another, not a change in the form itself adapted of course to its *own* advantage - since natural laws, forces, and conditions

of environment could not conceivably *design* the advantage of another form, and cause one to change for the benefit of that other.

Why is it, again, that crabs and crayfish can only grow by casting off their shells, during which process they often die, as well as remain exposed defenceless to the attacks of enemies? Why should stags shed their horns also, leaving them defenceless for a time? Other animals do not do so, and there is nothing in the nature of the horn which requires it.

This brief allusion is here sufficient. Mr. Mivart's work gives it at large.

(2) Passing next to the question of the advantage of *incomplete stages* - portions of a mechanism only useful when complete, the most striking examples may be found in the Vegetable kingdom. The fertilization of flowering plants is effected by the pollen, a yellow dust formed in the anthers, which is carried from flower to flower. In the pines and oaks, this is done by the wind. But in other cases insects visit a flower to get the honey, and in so doing get covered with pollen, which they carry away and leave in the next flower visited. Now one of our commonest and most useful plants, the red clover, is so constructed that it can only be fertilized by humble bees. If this bee became extinct, the plant would die out; how can such a development be advantageous to it?

But the contrivances by which this process of fertilization is secured are so marvellous, that I confess I am completely staggered by the idea that these contrivances have been caused by the self-growth and adaptation of the plant without guidance. There is a plant called *Salvia glutinosa*[1] - easily recognized by its sticky calyx and pale yellow flowers. The anthers that bear the pollen are hidden far back in the hood of the flower, so that the pollen can neither fall nor can the wind carry it away; but the two anthers are supported on a sort of spring, and directly a bee goes to the flower and pushes in his head to get the honey, the spring is depressed and both anthers start forward, of course depositing their pollen on the hairy back of the bee, which carries it to the stigma of the next flower. This process can be tested without waiting for a bee, by pushing a bit of stick into the flower, when the curious action described will be observed. It is very easy to say that this admirable mechanical contrivance is of great use to the plant *in its complete* form; but try and imagine what use an intermediate form would have been! If development at once proceeded to the complete form, surely this marks *design*; if not, no partial step towards it would have been of any use, and therefore would not have been inherited and perpetuated so as to prepare for further completion. But many other plants have a structure so marvellous that this objection is continually applicable. Let me only recall one other case, that of the orchid, called *Coryanthes macrantha*. In this flower there are two little horns, which secrete a pure water, or rather water mixed with honey. The lower part of the flower consists of a long lip, the end of which is bent into the form of a bucket hanging below the horns. This bucket catches the nectar as it drops, and is furnished with a spout over which the liquid trickles when it is too full. But the mouth of the bucket is guarded by a curiously ridged cover with two openings, one on each side. The most ingenious man, says Mr. Darwin, would never by himself make out what this elaborate arrangement was intended for. It was at last discovered. Large humble bees were seen visiting the flower; by way of getting at the honey, they set to work to gnaw off the ridges of the lid above alluded to; in doing this they pushed one another into the bucket, and had to crawl out by the spout. As they passed out by this narrow aperture, they had to rub against the anthers and so carried off the pollen. When a bee so charged gets into another bucket, or into the same bucket a second time, and has to crawl out, he brushes against the stigma, and leaves the pollen on it. I might well have adduced this plant as another instance of the first objection, since it may well be asked, How could such a development, resulting in a structure which presents the greatest difficulty in the way of fertilization, be beneficial to the plant? But here the point is that, even if any one could assert the utility of such an elaborate and complicated development, and suppose it self-caused by accident or effect of environment, it certainly goes against the idea that all forms are due to an *accumulation of small changes*. For these curious contrivances in the case of *Salvia, Coryanthes,* and other plants, would in any case have been no use to the plant till the whole machinery *was complete*. Now, on the theory of slow changes gradually accumulating till the complete result was attained, there must have been generation after generation of plants, in which the machinery was as yet imperfect and only partly built up. But in such incomplete stages, fertilization would have been impossible, and therefore the plant must have died out. Just the same with the curious fly-trap in *Dionoea*. Whatever may be its benefit to the plant, till the whole apparatus as it now is, was *complete*, it would have been of no use. In the animal kingdom also, instances might be given: the giraffe has a long neck which is an advantage in getting food that other animals cannot reach; but what would have been the use of a neck which was becoming - and had not yet become - long? here intermediate stages would not have been useful, and therefore could not have been preserved.[2] In flat fishes it is curious that, though they are born with eyes on different sides of the head, the lower eye gradually grows round to the upper-side. As remarked by Mr. Mivart, natural selection could not have produced this change, since the *first* steps towards it could have been of no possible use, and could not therefore have occurred, at least not without direction and guidance from without. Mr. Darwin's explanation of the case does not touch this difficulty.

(3) The third point, the occurrence of so much *beauty* in organic life, is perhaps one of the most conclusive arguments for design in nature.

Here, if possible, more clearly than elsewhere, I see a total failure of "natural causes." We are told that the beauty of birds (for instance) is easily accounted for by the fact, that the ornamented and beautiful males are preferred by the other sex; and that this is an advantage, so the beauty has been perpetuated; and the same with butterflies and beetles.

We are told also that bright-coloured fruits attract birds, who eat the soft parts of the fruit and swallow the hard stone or seed which is thus prepared for germination, and carried about and dispersed over the earth's surface. Again, showy coloured flowers attract insects, which carry away pollen and fertilize other flowers.

All this is perfectly true; but it entirely fails to go far enough to meet the difficulty.

Now passing over such difficulties as the fact that bright colours in flowers *do not* attract insects in many cases, but much more inconspicuous flowers if they have a scent (mignonette, for example) *do*; passing over such a fact as that afforded by the violet, which (as some may not be aware) has two kinds of flower, one scented and of a beautiful colour, the other green and inconspicuous, and it is the *latter, not the former* which is usually fertile; - passing over all detailed difficulties of this kind, I allude only to the one great one, that in all these cases, besides mere bright colour, conspicuousness or showiness, there is a great and wonderful beauty of pattern, design, or colour arrangement, in nature. Now there is not a particle of evidence to show that any animal has, to the smallest extent, a *sense of beauty*. On the contrary it is most improbable. The sense of artistic beauty is not only peculiar to man, but only exists in him when civilized and cultivated. Uneducated people among ourselves have no sense of landscape and other beauty. How then can it exist in animals?

If there was nothing to explain but a uniform bright and showy colour, natural selection might be sufficient to account for it. How is it, then, that this is not the case? We have not only colour, but colour diversified in the most elaborate and charming manner. Look at the exquisite patterns on a butterfly's wing! look at the various delicate arrangements of colour and pattern in flowers; or look again at the arrangement of colour on a humming-bird - sometimes the tail, sometimes the breast is ornamented, sometimes a splendid crest covers the head, sometimes a jewelled gorget or ruff surrounds the throat; and these are not uniformly coloured, but exhibit metallic and other changes of lustre not to be imitated by the highest art. But to fully realize this, I had best refer to a more familiar instance. Let any one examine - as an object very easily procurable in these days - a peacock's feather. No doubt the whole tail when expanded is very brilliant; but look closely at the structure of a single feather; is all this arrangement needed only to make the tail bright or conspicuous? Observe how wonderfully the outer parts are varied; part has a metallic lustre of copper, part has this also shot with green: then there is a delicate ring of violet with a double yellowish border, all quite distinct from the inmost gorgeous "eye" of green, blue, and black, and all arranged on the same feather!

Take, again, the so-called diamond beetle of Brazil; here the wing case is black studded all over with little pits or specks, which as a whole only give it a powdery pale-green colour; but place it in the sunlight and look at it with a magnifying glass - each little speck is seen to be furnished with a set of minute metallic scales showing green and red flashes like so many diamonds. How does such a delicate ornament answer the demands of mere conspicuousness?

But there is a stronger case than this. I before alluded to the exquisite symmetry of the silicious and crystalline coverings of some of the simplest forms of marine animalcules; and also I may here add the beautiful colouring of *shells* sometimes on the *inside*.[1] In what possible way would this beauty serve for any purely *useful* purpose?

Lastly, how are we to account for the beauty of autumnal tints in woods, or coloured *leaves* in plants such as the *Caladium*? The beauty is of no conceivable use to the plant.

"In Canada the colours of the autumn forest are notorious. Even on cloudy days the hue of the foliage is of so intense a yellow that the light thrown from the trees creates the impression of bright sunshine, each leaf presents a point of sparkling gold. But the colours of the leafy landscape change and intermingle from day to day, until pink, lilac, vermilion, purple, deep indigo and brown, present a combination of beauty that must be seen to be realized; for no artist has yet been able to represent, nor can the imagination picture to itself, the gorgeous spectacle.[1]"

Have we not here an exhibition which cannot be accounted for on any principle of natural utility?

(4) The fourth point, as previously stated, will be best treated by stating beforehand what is the conclusion come to, and then justifying it. My suggestion is that if we suppose a continuous evolution without a series of designs prescribed before life began to develop, and without any external guidance, then we are lost in difficulties. We cannot account for why variation should set in in the very different ways it does, nor why such a vast variety of divergent results should be produced. We cannot account for the tendency to reversion to a previous type, when artificial or accidental variation is not continually maintained,[1] nor for the sterility of hybrids; nor, above all, for evolution performing such freaks (if I may so say) as the origination of our small finches and the tropical humming-birds from earlier vertebrates through the Mesozoic reptiles, the pterodactyles, *Odontornithes* and subsequent forms. Supposing that the Almighty Designer created a complete *cosmos* of (1) the starry heavens and the planetary system, (2) then a scheme whereby earth and water were to be duly distributed

over our planet; (3) established the relations by which the external heavenly bodies were to regulate our seasons, tides, and times (as we know they do). (4) Suppose, further, that the Designer did not make "out of nothing" the series of finally developed animals as we now have them, but "made the animals make themselves" - that is to say, created the type, the ideal form, and adapted the laws and forces which constitute environment, so that development of form should go on regularly towards the appointed end, but in separate and appropriate channels, each terminating when its object had been attained. Suppose these conditions (which, as we shall afterwards see, are what Revelation, fairly interpreted, declares) to exist; all the known *facts*, and also the fairly certain *inferences* of Evolution, are then accounted for.

We have neither by revelation nor physical discovery an exact *scheme* of all the types, nor which of the elementary forms were destined to remain unchanged throughout. But some scheme of created types we surely have. Whether what we call *species*[1] are all types or not, we cannot say; probably not. All we can be sure of is that there are definite lines somewhere. We see the sterility of some hybrids, for instance, which would seem to indicate that while some forms can conjugate and their offspring remain fertile, others (approaching, as it were, the verge of separation) give rise to hybrids which are or not absolutely sterile,[2] according as they approach, or are more remote from, the designed barrier-line. And at that point the separation is insuperable. Certain forms of *Carnivora* and *Ungulata* seem to be for ever apart - not only the two great orders, but even subdivisions within them. Reptiles and birds, on the other hand, unlike as they at first sight seem, have no type line drawn to separate them; that, at least, is one of the more recent conclusions of biological science.

In other cases where variation has occurred, and especially when it is artificially - i.e., by the aid of selective breeding - caused or favoured, there is the constant tendency to *revert*, which is at once intelligible if there is a type scheme to be maintained.

If there were a series of created types, there may naturally have been what I may call sub-types; which would be certain well-marked stages on the way to the final form. Such sub-type forms would naturally occur at different ages, and being marked would show their place in the scale, and their connection with the ultimate perfect form. Such a possibility would exactly account for the series of *Eohippus, Hipparion*, and horse, which we have already instanced; and still more so for the rise and disappearance of the great Mesozoic Saurians when their object was fulfilled. Deny guidance and type, and everything becomes confused. Why should variation take certain directions? how comes it that natural forces and conditions of life so occur and co-operate as to produce the variety of changes needed?

And there is also one other general objection which I desire to state.

Why should *development* have gone in different directions *towards the same object*? I grant that different circumstances would produce different changes, but not for the same purpose. For example take eye-sight. The world shows several types of eye. The *insect* eye quite unlike any other; the crustacean eye also distinct; and birds, fishes, and animals having an eye which is generally similar and is somewhat imitated by the eye of the *cuttle fish* (which is not a *fish*, but a *cephalopod*).

Again, granted that *poison* is a useful defence to creatures: how is it given so differently? - to a serpent in the tooth; to a bee or a scorpion in the tail; to a spider in a specially adapted *antenna*, and to the centipede in a pair of modified legs on the *thorax*.

One would have supposed that natural causes tending to produce poison weapons would have all gone on the same lines. And, curiously, in some few cases, we have a sameness of line. About twelve species - all fish - have an electric apparatus, familiar to most of us in the flat sea-fish called *Torpedo* and in the fresh-water eel called *Gymnotus*. The only answer the anti-creationist can give to this dissimilarity of development is that there are many vacant places in the polity of nature, and that development takes place in that direction which fits the creature to occupy a vacant place, and is, therefore, diverse.

It seems to me that this - the only answer that can he given - is necessarily a modified form or mode *of creation.* How can *natural causes* know anything about a polity of nature and a vacant place, here and there, so that the creature must develop in one way or another to fill it?

Another set of cases is the production of similar functional results by most diverse means, as in the case of flying animals, birds, pterodactyles, and bats; here there is a widely different modification of the fore-arm and other bones, all for the same purpose. The reader will do well to refer to Mr. Mivart's book on this subject.

Again, the question of types seems to be pointed to in the curious fact of what I may call the double development of birds from reptiles. Mr. Mivart says, "If one set of birds sprang from one set of reptiles and another set from another set of reptiles, the two sets could never by 'natural selection' only have grown into such perfect similarity." Yet we can trace the *Struthious* birds (those that, like ostriches, do not fly) through the Dinosaurs and *Dinornis*, and the flying Carinate birds though pterodactyles, *Archaeopteryx*, and *Icthyornis*, &c.

It might well be added to this part of the subject, that granted that developmental changes were often small, that progress was attained little by little, this does not appear to have been always the case.

The discoveries of the fossil species of horse,[1] *Eohippus, Hipparion*, and so forth, clearly establish a developmental series, and the ancient forms are claimed as the ancestor of the modern horse; but these (Professor Owen tells us) differed more from one another than the ass and the zebra (for instance) differ from the horse. Still, of course it may be that there are still undiscovered intermediate forms; and in any case there need be no desire to detract from the value of the series, as really pointing towards a gradual perfection of the horse from a ruder ancestor up to the latest type. But having reached the type, and though that type exhibits such (considerable) variations as occur between the Shetland pony, the Arab, and the dray-horse, we have still no difficulty in recognizing the essential identity; nor is there any evidence or any probability that the horse will ever change into anything essentially different. All the fossil bats, again, were true bats: and so with the rhinoceroses and the elephants. Granting the fullest use that may be made of the imperfection of the geological record, it is difficult to account for this, and still more for the absence of intermediate forms (particularly suitable for preservation) of the *Cetaceae*. The Zeuglodons from Eocene down to Pliocene, the Dolphins in the Pliocene, and the *Ziphoids Catodontidae*, and *Balaenidae* in the Pliocene, are all fully developed forms, with no intermediate species.

Mr. Mivart remarks, "There are abundant instances to prove that considerable modifications may suddenly develop themselves, either due to external conditions or to obscure internal causes in the organisms which exhibit them.[1]" If it is not so, granted to the full the imperfection of the Geologic record, but remembering the cases where we *do* find intermediate forms; we ask why should they not be preserved in other cases? If they ever existed we should surely see *more* changing forms; not only such as are more or less uncertainly divided species, but whole orders running one into another. No evidence exists to show that any bird has gradually passed into an animal, nor a carnivorous beast become ruminant, or *vice versa.*

The analogy of changes that are known will not bear extension enough to prove, even probably, any such change.

Surely if our conclusion in favour of a Divine Design to be attained, and a Providential Intelligence directing the laws of development, is no more than a belief, it is a probable and reasonable belief: it certainly meets facts and allows place for difficulties in a way far more satisfactory than the opposite belief which rejects *all* but "secondary" and purely "natural" causes.

So clear does this seem to me, that I cannot help surmising that we should never have heard of any objection to Divine creation and providential direction, if it had not been for a prevalent fixed idea, that by "creation" *must* be meant a final, one-act production *(per saltum)* of a completely developed form, where previously there had been nothing. Such a "creation" would of course militate against *any* evolution, however cautiously stated or clearly established. And no doubt such an idea of "creation" was and still is prevalent, and would naturally and almost inevitably arise, while nothing to the contrary in the *modus operandi* of Creative Power was known. What is more strange is that the current objection should not now be, "Your *idea of creation* is all wrong," rather than the one which has been strongly put forward (and against which I am contending), "There is no place for a Creator."

(5) This is the only other *general* point that remains to be taken up in connection with the theory that all living forms are due to the gradual accumulation of small favourable changes without creative intervention. The objection is that we cannot obtain the inconceivably long time required for the process of uncontrolled and unaided evolution.

I am not here concerned to argue generally for the shortness or longness of the periods of geological time; let us, for the purposes of argument, admit a very wide margin of centuries and ages; but *some* limit there must be. The sun's light and heat, for one thing, are necessary, and though the bulk of combustible material in the sun is enormous, there must be some end to it. Sir William Thomson has calculated (and his calculations have never been answered) that on purely physical grounds, the existence of life on the earth must be limited to some such period as 100 millions of years; and this is far too short for uncontrolled evolution.

We know from fossils, that species have remained entirely unaltered since the glacial epochs began, and how many generations are included even in that! If no change is visible in all that time, how many more ages must have elapsed before a primitive *Amoeba* could have developed into a bird or a Mammal?

In Florida Mr. Agassiz has shown that coral insects exist unchanged, and must have been so for 30,000 years.

When we remember also the enormous destruction of life that takes place, supposing that in a given form a few creatures underwent accidental changes which were beneficial and likely to aid them - still what chances were there that the creatures which began to exhibit the right sort of change should have died before they left offspring! the chances against them are enormous: and the chances have to be repeated at every successive change before the finally perfected or advanced creature took its place in the polity of nature. Moreover, there is the chance of small changes being lost by intercrossing: our own cattle-breeders have most carefully to select the parents, or else the favourable variety soon disappears.

How then, seeing the power of stability which at least some forms are found to exhibit - seeing too the enormous chances against the survival of the particular specimens that begin to vary, and the further chances of the loss of variety by intercrossing; how can we get the millions of millions of years necessary to produce the present extreme divergence of species? The fact is that the force of this objection is likely to be undervalued, from the mere difficulty of bringing home to the mind the immeasurable time really demanded by uncontrolled evolution.

Nor is the question of time left absolutely to be matter of belief or speculation. For here and there in the geological records of the rocks, we *have* certain intermediate forms - or forms which we may fairly argue to be such. But looking at the very considerable differences between the earlier and the later of these forms - differences greater than those which now separate well-defined species, it seems questionable whether any of the divisions of Tertiary time, taking all the circumstances into consideration, could be lengthened out sufficiently to accomplish the change.

At any rate, if any particular example be disallowed, the general objection must be admitted to be weighty.

Now the intervention of any system of created designs of animal form - however little its details be understood - and the production of variations under *divine guidance* which would lead more directly to the accomplishment of such forms as the complicated flowers of orchids above described, would unquestionably tend to shorten the requisite time. There would, by a process of reasoning easily followed, be an immediate reduction of the ages required, within practicable limits, though the time must still remain long. More than that is not necessary. The Ussherian chronology is not of Divine revelation, though some persons speak of it as if it was. There is not the shadow of a reason to be gleaned from the Bible, nor from any other source, that the commencement of orderly development, the separation of land and water, earth and sky, and the subsequent provision of designs for organic forms of life and the first steps that followed the issue of the design, began six thousand years ago, or anything like it. It can be shown, indeed, that *historical* man, or the specific origin of the man spoken of as Adam, dates back but a limited time; and it is calculable with some degree of probability how far; but that is all. We are therefore in no difficulty when ample time is demanded; but we are in the greatest straits when the illimitable demands of a slowly and minutely stepping development, perpetually liable to be checked, turned back, and even obliterated, have to be confronted with other weighty probabilities and calculations regarding the sun's light and heat, and the duration of particular geologic eras.

CHAPTER VII.

THE DESCENT OF MAN.

We now approach a special objection which always, has been (and I shall be pardoned, perhaps, for saying *always will be*) the *crux* of the theory of unaided, uncreated evolution - the advent of reasoning, and not only reasoning, but self-conscious and God-conscious MAN.

Here again the lines of argument are so numerous, and the details into which we might go so varied, that a rigid and perhaps bald selection of a few topics is all that can be attempted.

But I may remark that naturalists are far from being agreed on this part of the subject. Agassiz rejects the evolution of man altogether. Mr. St. G. Mivart, while partly admitting, as every one else now does, the doctrine of evolution, denies the descent of man. Mr. Wallace, the great apostle of evolution, opposes Darwin, and will have none of his views on the descent of man; and Professor Huxley himself says that, while the resemblance of structure is such that if any "process of physical causation can be discovered by which the genera and families of ordinary animals have been produced, the process of causation is amply sufficient to account for the origin of man," still he admits that the gulf is vast between civilized man and brutes, and he is certain that "whether *from* them or not, man is assuredly not *of* them."

The first difficulty I shall mention is, however, a structural one. Supposing that an ape-like ancestor developed into man, on the principles of natural selection; then his development has taken place in a manner directly contrary to the acknowledged law of natural selection. He has developed backwards; his frame is in every way weaker; he is wanting in agility; he has lost the prehensile feet; he has lost teeth fitted for fighting or crushing or tearing; he has but little sense of smell; he has lost the hairy covering, and is obliged to help himself by clothes.[1] If this loss was ornamental it is quite unlike any other development in this respect, since no other creature has the same; for ornamental purposes the fur becomes coloured, spotted, and striped, but not lost. It is easy to reply that man being *intelligent*, his brain power enables him to invent clothes, arms, implements, and so forth, which not only supply all deficiencies of structure, but give him a great superiority over all creatures. But how did he get that intelligence? By what natural process of causation (without intelligent direction) is it conceivable that, given a species of monkey, all at once and at a certain stage, structural development should have been retarded and actually reversed, and a development of brain structure alone set in? Nor, be it observed, has any trace of *man* with a rudimentary brain ever been discovered. Savages have brains far in excess of their requirements, and can consequently be educated and improved. The skull of a prehistoric man found in the Neanderthal near Dusseldorf is of average brain capacity, showing that in those remote ages man was very much in capacity what he is at present.

It must, however, be admitted that the special difficulties of the origin of man are not purely structural. We do not know enough of the Divine plan to be able to understand why it is that there is a certain undeniable unity of form, in the two eyes, ears, mouth, limbs and organs generally of the animal and man. Moreover, much is made of the fact, as stated by a recent "Edinburgh Reviewer," that "the physical difference between man and the lowest ape is trifling compared with that which exists between the lowest ape and any brute animal that is not an ape.[1]" This fact no doubt negatives the idea put forward by Bishop Temple and others, that if there was an evolution of man, it must have been in a special branch which was foreseen and commenced very far back in the scale of organic being. For the structural difference might not require such a separate origin; while the mental difference, affording objections of a different class, will not allow of *any* such evolution at all. That there is *some* connection between man and the animal cannot be denied, and consequently, in the absence of fuller information, very little would be gained by insisting on the purely *physical* development question. The Bible states positively that the man Adam (as the progenitor of a particular race, at any rate) was a separate and actual production, on a given part of the earth's surface. All that we need conclude regarding that is that there is nothing known which entitles us to say, "This is not a fact, and therefore is not genuine revelation."

Moreover, as to the question of the possibility of human development generally, there are certain considerations which directly support our belief. For example, directly we look to the characteristic point, the gift of intellect, we can reasonably argue that the action of a Creator is indispensable. The entrance of consciousness and of reason, however elementary, marks something out of all analogy with the development of physical structure, just as much as the entrance of Life marked a new departure in no analogy with the "properties" of inorganic matter.

From the first dawn of what looks like *will* and *choice* between two things, and something like a *reason* which directs the course of the organism in a particular way for a particular object, we have an altogether new departure. The difficulty commences at the outset, and even in the animal creation; it is merely continued and rendered more striking when we take into consideration the higher development of intellect into power of abstract reasoning, self-consciousness and God-consciousness.

It is perfectly true that the difference between the "instinct" of animals and the reason and mind of man, is one of degree rather than kind. As Christians, we have no objection whatever to a development of reason from the lowest reason solely concerned with earthly and bodily affairs to the highest powers searching into deep and spiritual truths. But such a development, though it is parallel to a physical development - as spiritual law appears to be always parallel (as far as the nature of things permits) to physical laws - still is a development which cannot under any possible circumstances dispense with an external spiritual order of existence, and one which cannot be physically caused. Nor is it conceivable that man should develop a consciousness of God, when no God really exists externally to the consciousness.[1]

The main objection, then, that I would press is, that admitting any possibility of the development of man from a purely physical and structural point of view, admitting any inference that may be drawn fairly from the undoubted connection (increasingly great as it is as we go upwards from the lower animal to the ape) between animals and man, that inference never can touch the descent of man as a whole; because no similarity of bodily structure can get over the difficulty of the mental power of man. We have to deal not with a part of man, but with the whole. The difficulty cannot be got over by denying *mind* as a thing *per se*; for all attempts to represent mind as the *mere* product of a physical structure, the brain, utterly fail.

Nobody wishes to deny what Dr. H. Maudsley and others have made so plain to us, that mind has (in one aspect, at any rate) a physical basis - that is, that no thought, imagination, or combination of thought, is known to us *apart from* change and expenditure of energy in the brain. Nor can we, by any process of introspection or observation of other subjects, separate the mind from the brain and ascertain the existence of "pure mind," or soul, experimentally. But still, there is no possibility of getting the operations of mind out of mere cell structure, unless an external Power has added the mind power, as a faculty of His endowing; then He may be allowed to have connected that faculty ever so mysteriously with physical structure; we are content. And I must insist on the total failure of all analogy between the development of bones or muscles and the development of mind; and even if we grant a certain stage of instinct to have arisen, we are still in the dark as to how that could develop into intellect such as man possesses, including a belief in God. On this subject let us hear Professor Allman. Between a development of material structure and a development of intellectual and moral features, the Professor says, "there is no conceivable analogy; and the obvious and continuous path, which we have hitherto followed up, in our reasonings from the phenomena of lifeless matter to those of living form, here comes suddenly to an end. The chasm between *unconscious* life and *thought* is deep and impassable, and no transitional phenomena are to be found by which, as by a bridge, we can span it over.[1]"

There can be *life* or *function* without *consciousness* or *thought;* therefore, even if we go so far as to admit that life is only a property of protoplasm, there can be no ground for saying that *thought* is only a property of protoplasm.

"If," says Professor Allman, "we were to admit that every living cell were a conscious and thinking thing, are we therefore justified in asserting that its consciousness with its irritability is a property of the matter of which it is composed? The sole argument on which this view is made to rest is analogy. It is argued that because the life phenomena, which are invariably found in the cell, must be regarded as a property of the cell, the phenomena of consciousness by which they are accompanied must also be so regarded. The weak point in the argument is the absence of all analogy between the things compared: and as the conclusion rests solely on the argument from analogy, the two must fall to the ground together."

Try and assign to matter all the properties you can think of, its impenetrability, extension, weight, inertia, elasticity, and so forth, by no process of thought (as Mr. Justice Fry observes in an article in "The Contemporary Review [1]") can you get out of them an adequate account of the phenomena of mind or spirit.

We just now observed that consciousness, thought, and so forth, are never exhibited apart from the action of the brain; some change in the brain accompanies them all. We do not deny that. But it is obvious that thought being manifested in the presence of cerebral matter or something like it, is a very different thing from thought being a *property* of such matter, in the sense in which polarity is the property of a magnet, or irritability of living protoplasm.

To all this I have seen no answer. The way in which the opponents of Christian beliefs meet such considerations appears to be to ignore or minimize them, so as to pass over to what seems to them a satisfactory if not an easy series of transitions. If Life is after all only a "property" of matter, then given life, a brain may be produced; and as mind is always manifested in the presence of (and apparently indissolubly united with) brain structure, it is not a much greater leap to accept *life* as a property of *matter* than it is to take *thought* as a property of a certain *specialized physical structure*. It is true that the distance is great between the instinct of an animal and the abstract reasoning power of a Newton or a Herbert Spencer; but (as we are so often told) the difference is of degree not of kind, and as the brain structure develops, so does the power and degree of reason. As to the difference in man, that he is the only "religious" animal - the one creature that has the idea of God - that is a mere development of the emotions in connection with abstract reasoning as to the cause of things. No part of our mental nature is more common to the animal and the man than the emotional; and if in the one it is mere love and hatred, joy and grief, confidence and fear, in the other the emotions are developed into the poetic sense of beauty, or the awe felt for what is grand and noble; and this insensibly passes into *worship*, the root of the whole being fear of the unknown and the mysterious. That is the general line of argument taken up.

Even accepting the solution (if such it maybe called) of the two first difficulties - life added spontaneously or aboriginally to matter, and thought and consciousness added to organism - still the rest of the path is by no means so easy as might at the first glance appear. Development in brain structure certainly does not always proceed *pari passu* with a higher and more complex reasoning. In actual fact we find high "reasoning" power, quite unexpectedly here and there, up and down the animal kingdom. Some *insects*, with very little that can be called a brain at all, exhibit high intelligence; and some animals with smaller brains are more docile and intelligent than others with a much larger development. The ape, in spite of his close physical approach to the structure of man, and his still greater relative distance from the other animal creation, is not superior (if he is not decidedly inferior) in reason or intelligence to several animals lower down in the scale.

Savages, again, have a brain greatly in excess of their actual requirements (so to speak). Hence the mere existence of brain, however complex, does not indicate the possession of mental power.

There is reason to believe that all thought and exercise of the mind - in fact, every step in the process of "Education," whereby an ignorant person is brought at last to apprehend the most abstract propositions - is accompanied by some molecular (or other) change. So that a person who has been carefully educated has the brain in a different state from that of an exactly similarly constituted person whose brain has been subjected to no such exercise. But even if this action could be formulated and explained, it would not follow that thought is the *product* of the molecular change; or that, *vice versa*, if we could artificially produce certain changes, in the brain, certain thoughts and perceptions would thereon coexist with the changes, and arise in the mind of the subject forthwith. And if not, then no process of physical development accounts for grades of intellect; we have only mind developing as mind. But the theory of evolution will have nothing to do with any development but physical; or at any rate with mental development except as the result of physical: it knows nothing of pure mind, or spiritual existence, or anything of the sort.

In the nature of things we can have neither observation nor experiment in this stage. We cannot by any process develop the lower mind of an animal into the higher mind of man, and prove the steps of the evolution.[1] It is important to remember that the power of *directing the attention by a voluntary process of abstraction*, is one that distinctively belongs to man. It is an effort of will, of a kind that no animal has any capacity for. By it alone have we any power of abstract reasoning, and it is intimately concerned with our self-consciousness and memory, and with our language. I am quite aware that animals possess something analogous to a language of their own; they can indicate certain emotions and give warning, and so forth, to their fellows. But that language could never develop into human language, or the animal will (such as it is) ever rise to a human will, or animals become endowed with self-consciousness, unless they could acquire the power of voluntarily abstracting the mind from one subject or part of a subject and fixing the attention on another. We cannot formulate any process of change whereby the lower state could pass on to or attain to the higher in this respect.

Therefore again we conclude that the higher reason is a gift *ab externo*.

If we take a step further to the "spiritual" or "moral" faculties of man, we have the same difficulty intensified, if indeed it does take a new departure. To examine the question adequately would require us to go into the deep waters of psychology; and here we should encounter many matters regarding which there may be legitimate doubt and difference of opinion, which would obscure and lead us away from our main line of thought.

This I would willingly avoid. But it is quite intelligible, and touches on no dangerous ground, when we assert that there is a distinct ascent - an interval again raising developmental difficulties, directly we pass from the intellectual to the moral. We may wonder at the high degree of intelligence possessed by some animals; but we are unable to conceive any animal possessing a power of abstract reasoning, having ideas of beauty (as such), or of manifesting what we call the poetic feeling. And still more is this so when we look at the further interval that lies between any perception of physical phenomena, any reasoning in the abstract, or investigation of mathematical truth, and the overmastering sense of obligation to the "moral law," or the action of the soul in its instinctive possession of the conception of a Divine Existence external to itself. It is because of this felt difference that we talk of the "spiritual" as something beyond and above the "mental."

The distinction is real, though we must not allow ourselves to be led too far in attempting to scan the close union that, from another point of view, exists between the one and the other.

In a recent number of "The Edinburgh Review,[1]" the author complains of Bishop Temple thus: "He uses the word spiritual in such a way that he might be taken to imply that we had some other faculty for the perception of moral truths, in addition to, and distinct from, our reason." And the writer goes on to make an "uncompromising assertion of reason as the one supreme faculty of man. To depreciate reason (he says) to the profit of some supposed 'moral' illative sense, would be to open the door to the most desolating of all scepticisms, and to subordinate the basis of our highest intellectual power to some mere figment of the imagination."

On the other hand, some writers (claiming to derive their argument from the Scriptures) have supposed they could assert three distinct natures in man - a spiritual, a mental (or psychic), and a bodily. Now there is no doubt that, rightly or wrongly (I am not now concerned with that), the Bible does distinctly assert that a "breath of lives" [1] was specially put into the bodily form of man, and adds that thereby "man became a living soul." But it is also stated of the animal creation that the breath of life was given to them,[2] and animals are said to have a "soul" (nephesh).[3] So that neither in the one case nor the other have we more than the two elements: a body, and a life put into it; though of course the man's "life" (as the plural indicates, and other texts explain) was higher in kind than that of the animal.

St. Paul, it is true, speaks of the "whole spirit, and soul, and body.[1]" But our Lord Himself, in a very solemn passage (where it would be most natural to expect the distinction, if it were absolute and structural, to be noticed), speaks of the "soul and body" only.[2]

The fact is that we are only able to argue conclusively that, besides the physical form, we have a non-material soul, or a self. And our Lord, whose teaching was always eminently practical, went no further. We are conscious of a "self" - something that remains, while the body continually grows and changes.

There was in *Punch*, some time ago, a picture of an old grandfather, with a little child looking at a marble bust representing a child. "Who is that?" asks the little one; and the old man replies, "That is grandfather when he was a little boy." "And who is it now?" rejoins the child. One smiles at the picture, but in reality it conceals a very important and a very pathetic truth. Nothing could well be greater than the outward difference between the grey hairs and bowed figure and the little cherub face; and yet there was a "self" - a soul, that remained the same throughout. In Platonic language, while the [Greek: eidolon] perpetually changes, the [Greek: eidos] remains. We have, therefore, evidence as positive as the nature of the subject admits that we are right in speaking of the *body and the soul, or self*. And as we cannot connect the higher reasoning, and, above all, conscience and the religious belief, as a "property" of physical structure, we conclude that the Scripture only asserts facts when it attributes both to the soul, as a spiritual element or nature belonging to the body. Man is essentially one;[3] but there is both a material and a non-material, a physical and a spiritual element, in the one nature.

But, being a spiritual element, that part of our nature necessarily has two sides (so to speak). It has its point of contact with self and the world of sense, and its point of contact with the world of spirit and with the Great Spirit of all, from whom it came. *Because* of that higher "breath of lives" given by the Most High, man possesses the faculty of *consciousness of God* (i.e., the higher spiritual faculties), besides the consciousness of self, or merely intellectual power regarding self and the external world. Therefore, when an Apostle desires to speak very forcibly of something that is to affect a man through and through, in every part and in every aspect of his nature, he speaks of the "whole spirit, soul, and body." To sum up: all that we know from the Bible is that God gave a "soul" (nephesh) to the animals, in consequence of which (when united to the physical structure) the functions of life and the phenomena of intelligence are manifested. So God gave a non-material, and therefore "spiritual," element to human nature; and this being of a higher grade and capacity to that of the animal world, not only in its union with physical structure, makes the man a "living soul" - gives him an intelligence and a certain reason such as the animals have, but also gives him, as a special and unique endowment; the consciousness of self (involving - which is very noteworthy - a consciousness of its own limitations) and the consciousness of God. Hence man's power of improvement. If the man cultivates only the self-consciousness and the reason that is with it, the Scriptures speak of him as the "natural or psychic man;" if he is enabled by Divine grace to develop the higher moral and spiritual part of his nature, and to walk after the Spirit, not after the flesh, he is a "spiritual man."

It is idle to speculate whether the "nephesh" of the

animals, or the "living self" of the man, is an entity separate from the body, and capable of existing *per se* - of its own inherent nature - apart from it. We do not know that animal forms are the clothing of a lower-graded but separate spiritual form, or that such an animal soul or spirit can exist separately from the body; and we do not *know* (from the Bible) - whatever may be the current language on the subject - that man's spirit is in its nature capable of anything like permanent separate existence.[1] Man is essentially one; and when the physical change called death passes over him, it does not utterly obliterate the whole being. The non-material element is not affected any more than it is by the sleep of every night; and the man will be ultimately raised, not a spiritual or immaterial form, but provided, as before, with a body, only one of a higher capacity and better adapted to its higher environments - the "spiritual body" of St. Paul, in a word. The original union of mind and matter is, on any possible theory, mysterious; and the separation of them for a time is neither less so, nor more. All this is perfectly true, whether the non-material element in man's nature is *necessarily*, inherently and *by nature*, immortal or not - a question which I do not desire to enter on.

Hence it is that a certain element of truth is recognized in the protest of the Edinburgh Reviewer. On the other hand, as we have not only intelligence, emotions (which are possessed in lower degree by animals), self-consciousness, the power of abstract reasoning, and the higher faculties of the imagination,[2] but also the consciousness of God and the commanding sense of right and wrong; and seeing that the last-named are different in kind from the former, we give them a separate name, and speak of the moral or spiritual nature or capacity of man, as well as the intellectual or mental. Some (by the way) choose "moral" to include both, holding that ethical perceptions arise out of (or are intimately connected with) our sense of God. Others would make a further distinction, and confine "moral" to the (supposed) bare ethical perception of duty or of right and wrong, and add "spiritual" to distinguish the highest faculty of all, whereby man holds communion with his Maker and recognizes his relation to Him.

Whether this further distinction is justified or not, there is a distinction between the moral and the purely intellectual; and we are justified in using different terms for things that are *practically* different. This the Edinburgh Reviewer seems to have forgotten.

It was necessary to my argument to enter on this somewhat lengthy examination of the spiritual nature of man, because, while we acknowledge the unity of man, we are compelled to recognize in his religious sense and aspirations and capacities something quite disparate - something that we could not get by a natural process of growth from such beginnings of reason as are observed in the lower animals.

I am aware that Dr. Darwin conceived that the religious feeling of man might have grown out of the natural emotions of fear,[1] love, gratitude, &c., when once men began to question as to the explanation of the phenomena of life, and to ascribe the forces of nature to the possession of a spirit such as he himself was conscious of: and with much more positive intent, Mr. H. Spencer has also, after most painstaking inquiries, formulated what he conceives to be the origin of religious belief in man. He refers us to the early belief in a "double" of self, which double could be projected out of self, and remained in some way after death, so as to become the object of fear, and ultimately of worship. When this ancestor-worship resulted in the worship of a multitude of "genii" (whose individuality, as regards their former earthly connection, is more or less forgotten), then the idea of attaching the numerous divinities or ancestor-souls to the ocean, the sky, the sun, the mountains, and the powers of nature, arises; whence the poetic systems of ancient polytheistic mythology. Gradually men began to reason and to think, and they refined the polytheism into the "higher" idea of one great, central, immaterial all-pervading power, which they called God.

Mr. Spencer, in effect, concludes that this "God" is only man's own idea of filling up a blank, of explaining the fact that there must be an ultimate first cause of whatever exists, and there is also a great source of power of some kind external to ourselves.[1]

I am not going here to enter on any special argument as to the validity of these theories in their relation to the direct question of the nature and existence of God. What we are here concerned with is, whether they enable us to exclude the idea of a gift and a giver of spiritual or mental (we will not quarrel about terms) nature to man, and whether, by any fair reasoning from analogy, we can suppose man's reason and his "*sensus numinis*" to arise by the mere stages of natural growth and development. Dr. Darwin's supposition takes no notice of the moral law and its influence; indeed he adopts[2] the view that conscience is no sense of right and wrong, but only the stored up and inherited social instinct, a sense of convenience and inconvenience to the tribe and to the individual, which at last acts so spontaneously and rapidly in giving its verdict on anything, that we regard it as a special sense. It would of course be possible to expend much time and many words in argument on this subject. There is not, and never will be, any direct evidence as to the origin of conscience; and as that sense (like any other power of our mental nature) is capable of being educated, evoked, enlightened, and strengthened, and may also by neglect and contradiction deteriorate and wither away, there is ample room for allowing a certain part of the theory.[3] But many people who examine their own conscience will feel that the description certainly does not suit them; there are many things which conscience disapproves, of which no great evil consequences to themselves or any one else are felt. Conscience is constantly condemning "the way that seemeth good unto a man." *Ultimately* no doubt, there is real evil at the end of everything that conscience warns a man against; but not such as "inherited experience" is likely to recognize. Is it, for instance, the experience of the mass of men, as men, that the "fleshly mind is death, but the spiritual mind is life and peace"? Is not rather the world at large habitually putting money-making, position-making, and the care of the things of the body, of time, and of sense, in the first place; and is not the moral law perpetually warning us that the fashion of the world passes away, and that what seems gold is in reality tinsel? As far as the condemnation that conscience passes on the broad evils which affect society - "thou shalt not steal," "thou shalt not lie," or so forth - no doubt it is supported by the transmitted sense of inconvenience; but who has told it of the evil of things that do not affect our social state? and who has changed the inconvenient, the painful, into the *wrong*? It is one thing to instinctively avoid a theft or a falsehood, even if the first origin of such instinct were the fear of consequences or the love of approbation; it is quite another - the inward condemnation of something which "the deceitfulness of sin" is able to excuse, and which the world at large would regard as permissible or at least venial. Even if inherited use has its full play, there is still a something wanted before the one can be got into (or out of) the other. Why, again, are savages prone to imagine natural phenomena to be caused or actuated by "spirits"? Surely it is because there *is* consciously a spirit in man, and a Higher Power, even God, outside, who exists, though man in his ignorance has many false ideas regarding Him.

It is an objection of the same order that applies to the other theory (Mr. Spencer's). There can be little doubt that in many respects it is true: as an account of all *human* systems of religion it is adequate and natural; but it breaks down hopelessly when we try to use it to explain how the conception of God originated in the mind. Just as there is a felt difference - not of degree or in form, but essential and radical in its nature - between the *undesirable* and the *wrong*, so there is a difference between the idea of a mysterious thing towards which apprehension or awe is felt, and the conception of God. Granted that man believed in his own spirit or double, and attributed similar immaterial motor powers as a cause for the wind and waves, and so forth; granted that he at last "refined" this into the belief in one Spirit whose power was necessarily great and varied - the origin is still unexplained. How did man get the idea of a personal spirit or double - no such thing, *ex hypothesi* existing? How did he get to formulate the idea of a *God* when he had simplified his group of many spirits into one?

If man is created with a consciousness of his own inner-self, *as a self*, he is able naturally to imagine a like self in other beings; if he has an idea of God innate in him, he can assimilate the truth when it is at last presented to his mind; and that is why he feels that it *is* a refinement; a rising from the lower to the higher (because from falsehood to truth), to let the many gods give place to the One God. If the idea of God has been obscured, and the power of its apprehension deadened, the man can only grope about helplessly, fashioning this explanation of nature and that - all more or less false, but all dimly bearing witness to the two absolute facts, that there is an inner non-material self, and an external non-material God.

If then there are insuperable difficulties in connecting thought with matter by any process of unaided development, there are also great difficulties, even when thought in a rudimentary form is given, in conceiving it developed into man's reason, or man's religious belief, by any known process of "natural" causation.

CHAPTER VIII.

FURTHER DIFFICULTIES REGARDING THE HISTORY OF MAN.

There are, however, some other matters connected with the history of man on the globe, unconnected with psychological development, but which demand notice, as making the argument against an undesigned, unaided development of man a cumulative one. It is urged that whatever may be thought of the connection of man with the animal creation, at any rate the received Christian belief regarding the origin of man - especially his late appearance on the scene - is contrary to known facts, and that we have to mount up to a vast geologic antiquity to account for what is known from exhumed remains in caves and lake dwellings, and the like.

Now no one pretends that the history of man is free from doubt and difficulty, but the doubt and difficulty are not confined to the "orthodox." For the inferences to be drawn from the exhumed remains are equally doubtful whatever views be adopted.

I shall not go into great length on this subject, partly because some recent popular tracts of Canon Rawlinson, Mr. R.S. Pattison, and others, have already made the ordinary reader familiar with the main outlines of the subject; and still more because, be the views of archaeologists what they may, it is impossible for any rational person to contend either that they can be reduced to anything like unity among themselves, or that they lead to any conclusion favourable to the belief in the self-caused and undesigned evolution of man.

It may be regarded as known, that at the dawn of history, mankind was passing through what may be called a Bronze age, in which weapons of bronze were used before tools of iron were invented. But this age was preceded by one in which even bronze was unknown. Stone implements, and some of bone and horn, were alone used. It is also well ascertained that there were two *widely divided* stone ages. The latter, distinguished by the polishing of the stones, is described as the *neolithic*; the former, in which flint and other hard stone fragments were merely chipped or flaked to an edge, is called the *palaeolithic*.

It is hardly contended that the neolithic age could have been more than four or five thousand years ago. There is always the greatest difficulty in fixing any dates because from the nature of the case written records are absent, and the stages of growth in the history of peoples overlap so.

We know that sharp flakes of stone were still used for knives in the time of Moses and Joshua. We are not out of the stone age yet, as regards some portions of the globe; and it is quite possible that parts of the earth, not so very remote, may have been still in the midst of a stone age when Assyria, Chaldaea, and Egypt were comparatively highly civilized.

It is also fairly certain that between the neolithic or smooth-stone age, and the palaeolithic, certain important geological changes took place, though those changes were not such as to have demanded any very great length of time for their accomplishment.

The palaeolithic stone implements are found in river gravels and clays, along the higher levels of our own Thames Valley, that of the Somme in France, and in other places. They are also found at the bottom of various natural caverns.

No human bones have been found as yet with the implements, but the bones of large numbers of animals have. And it seems certain that the men who made the implements were contemporaries of the animals, because in the later part of the age, at any rate, they drew or scratched likenesses of the animals on bone. Among these representations are figures of the *mammoth* an extinct form well known to the reader by description and museum specimens of remains.

The animals contemporary with these primeval men were the mammoth, species of rhinoceros and hippopotamus, the "sabre-toothed" lion, the cave-bear, the reindeer, besides oxen, horses, and other still surviving forms.

In his address to the British Association in 1881 Sir John Lubbock called attention to the fact that these animals appear to indicate both a hot and a cold climate, and he referred to the fact (known to astronomers) that the earth passes through periods of slow change in the eccentricity of its orbit, and in the obliquity of the ecliptic. The result of the latter condition is, to produce periods of about 21,000 years each, during one-half of which the Northern hemisphere will be hotter, and in the other the Southern. At present we are in the former phase.

But the obliquity of the ecliptic does not act alone; the eccentricity of the orbit produces another effect, namely, that when it is at a minimum the difference between the temperatures of the two hemispheres is small, and as the eccentricity increases, so does the difference. At the present time the eccentricity is represented by the fraction .016. But about 300,000 years ago the eccentricity would have been as great as .26 to .57. The result, it is explained, would have been not a uniform heat or cold, but extremes of both; there would probably have been short but very hot summers, and long and intensely cold winters.

This, Sir John Lubbock thought, might account for the co-existence of both hot and arctic species, like the hippopotamus and rhinoceros on the one hand, and the musk-ox and the reindeer on the other.

But such considerations really help us little. In the first place, it is only an assumption that the fossil hippopotamus *was* an animal of a hot climate - it does not in any way follow from the fact that the now existing species is such; nor if we make the assumption, does it explain how, if the hot summer sufficed for the tropical hippopotamus, it managed to survive the long and cold winters which suited the arctic species.

Moreover, no such calculations can really be made with accuracy: we do not know what other astronomical facts may have to be taken into consideration, nor can we say when such "periods" as those which are so graphically described, began or ended.

In this very instance, we know that the mammoth only became extinct in comparatively recent times, since specimens have been found in Siberia, with the hair, skin, and even flesh, entirely preserved. Granted that the intense cold of the Siberian ice effected this, it is impossible to admit more than a limited time for the preservation - not hundreds of thousands of years. Professor Boyd Dawkins is surely right in stating that the calculations of astronomy afford us no certain aid at present in this inquiry.

As regards the geological indications of age, the best authority seems to point to the first appearance of man in the post-glacial times: that is to say, that the gravels in which the palaeolithic implements are found were deposited by the action of fresh water after the great glacial period, when, at any rate, Northern Europe, a great part of Russia, all Scandinavia, and part of North America were covered with icefields, the great glaciers of which left their mark in the numerous scoopings out of ravines and lake beds and in the raising of banks and mounds, the deposit of boulders, and the striation of rocks *in situ*, which so many districts exhibit.

The few instances in which attempts have been made, in Italy or elsewhere, to argue for a pliocene man (i.e. in the uppermost group of the tertiary) have ended in failure, at least in the minds of most naturalists competent to judge.

One of the most typical instances of the position of the implement age has been discovered by Fraas at Shuessenried in Suabia; here the remains of tools and the bones of animals (probably killed for food) were found in holes made in the glacial *debris*.

But here, again, it is impossible to say when this glacial age terminated, and whether man might not have been living in other more favoured parts while it was wholly or partially continuing.

In Scandinavia no palaeolithic stone implements have been found, from which it may be inferred that the glacial period continued there during the ages when palaeolithic man hunted and dwelt in caves in the other countries where his remains occur.

The best authorities do not suppose that the men *originated* in the localities where the tools are found; and there is so little known about the geology of Central Asia (for example) that it is impossible to say whether tribes may not have wandered from some other places not affected by the glaciation we have spoken of.

Again, the gravels and brick earths containing the tools are just of the kind which defy attempts to say how long it took to deposit and arrange them.

It may be taken as certain, that after the one age ceased and the first men appeared, the beds in which their relics occur have been raised violently, and again depressed and subjected to great flushes and floods of water. The caves have been upheaved, and the gravels are found chiefly along the valleys of our present rivers, but at a much higher level, showing that there was both a higher level of the soil itself and a much greater volume of water.

The Straits of Dover were formed during this period.

But none of these changes required a very long time;

and if we can trace back the later stone age, which shows remains of pottery and other proofs of greater civilization, to the dawn of the historic period not more than 4000 or 5000 years ago, there is nothing in the nature of the changes which, as we have stated, intervened between the palaeolithic and neolithic periods, that need have occupied more than a thousand or two of years. Upheavals of strata and disruptions may be the work of but a short time, or they may be more gradual. And as to the effect of water, that depends on its volume and velocity; no certain rule can be given. Our own direct experience shows that very great changes may take place in a few hundred years.

"The estuaries," remarks Mr. Pattison,[1] "around our south-eastern coast, which have been filled up in historical times, some within the last seven hundred years to a height of thirty feet from their sea-level, by the gradual accumulation of soil, now look like solid earth in no way differing from the far older land adjoining. The harbours out of which our Plantagenet kings sailed are now firm, well-timbered land. The sea-channel through which the Romans sailed on their course to the Thames, at Thanet, is now a puny fresh-water ditch, with banks apparently as old as the hills. In Bede's days, in the ninth century, it was a sea-channel three furlongs wide."

Thus we are in complete uncertainty as to the date of the palaeolithic man, or as to the time necessary to effect the changes in the surface of the earth which intervened between it and the later stone ages. But there is nothing which conflicts with the possibility that the whole may have occurred within some 8,000 years.

For the supposition of Mons. Gabriel Mortillet that man has existed for 230,000 years, there is neither evidence nor probability. His theory is derived from an assumption that the geologic changes alluded to occupied an immense time; and the further assumption (if possible still more unwarranted) that the old race which used the chipped stone tools remained stationary for a very long period, and very gradually improved its tools and ultimately passed into the neolithic stage when the art of pottery became known, however rudely.

But, in point of fact, we are not required by our belief in Scripture to find any date for the origin of man, at least not within any moderate limits (not extending to scores of thousands of years). The Bible was not intended to enable us to construct a complete science of geology or anthropology, and the utmost that can be got out of the text is that a date can be *suggested* (not proved) for one particular family (that of Adam) by counting up the generations alluded to in Holy Writ before the time of Abraham. But these are manifestly recorded in a brief and epitomized form; nor do all the versions agree. We may well believe that a watchful Providence has taken care of the record of inspiration, but we know it has been done by human and ordinary agency. The Bible is God's gift to his Church, and the Church has been made in all ages the keeper of it. Now in the matter of early dates and numbers, an unanimous version has not been kept. According to the construction adopted in the Septuagint, the creation of Adam would go back 7,517 years, while the Vulgate gives 6,067 years. Dr. Hale's computation makes 7,294 years, and the Ussherian 5,967;[1] the Samaritan version is, I believe, further different from either.

As it is, the facts show nothing inconsistent with an approximation to these several periods.

As to any absolute date for the appearance of man as a species, no calculation is possible, because of a certain doubt, which no one can pretend to resolve, as to whether the Scriptures do assert the creation of *all* mankind at any one period. If, owing to more positive discoveries in the future compelling us to put further back the date of man's first appearance upon earth, we have to suppose a beginning before the time of Adam, we are reminded that there is an allusion in the sixth chapter of the book called Genesis to "the sons of God" and the "daughters of men." Now this passage cannot conceivably refer to angels; nor can we ignore its existence, however doubtful we may feel as to its meaning.[2]

It can hardly be denied that such a text opens out the *possibility* of an earlier race than that of Adam; in that case the creation of Adam would be detailed as the creation of the direct progenitor of Noah, whose three sons still give names (in ethnological language) to the main great races of the earth, with whom exclusively the Bible history is concerned, and especially as the direct progenitor of that race of whom came the Israelites, and in due time the promised seed - the Messiah. I do not say this *is* so, nor even that I accept the view for my own part; I only allude to the possibility, without ignoring any of the difficulties - none of which, however, are insuperable - which gather round it.

It is certainly a very remarkable fact that all about this region in which the Semitic race originated, traditions of Creation somewhat resembling the account in

Genesis, the institution of a week of seven days, and a Sabbath or day of rest from labour, existed from very early times; and with these traditions, a belief in distinct races, one of which owned a special connection with, or relation to, the Creator. Here I may appeal to the work of Mr. George Smith and his discoveries of tablets from the ancient libraries of Assyria. Originally, the country to which I have alluded consisted of Assyria in the centre and Babylonia to the south; while to the east of Assyria was a country partly plain and partly hill, which formed the "plain of Shinar" and the hills beyond occupied by Accadian tribes, from whose chief city, Ur, Abraham, the forefather of the Jews, emigrated. The Assyrian documents are copies of Babylonian originals, but the Babylonian kingdom itself was a Semitic one founded on the ruins of an earlier population, the inhabitants of the plain of Shinar and the mountains beyond. Some time between 3000 and 2000 B.C. the Semitic conquerors of Babylonia took possession of the plains, and some time later conquered also the Accadian mountaineers. The Babylonians possessed and translated the old Accadian records: the Assyrian tablets are mostly, but not all, copies, again, of the Babylonian transcripts. The celebrated "Creation tablets," which contain an account closely corresponding to Genesis, are among those which were not copied from Accadian originals; and they do not date further back than the reign of Assurbani-pal, the Sardanapalus of the Greeks; who reigned in the seventh century B.C. They may therefore be derived from the Bible, not the Bible from them. It would seem from some earlier (Accadian) tablets, that a different account of the Creation existed among them. But though it is doubtful how far the Accadians had preserved this account, or at least had others along with it, *they had a seven days week* and *a Sabbath*. All this points to *one* original tradition, which specified days of creation and a Sabbath, though it got altered and distorted, so that the true account was preserved as one among many local variations. This goes to prove the immense antiquity of the story, which is not affected by the fact that the actual inscription of it which we at present have, dates only about 670 B.C. The point here, however, interesting in the legends, is that they contained the idea of a special connection of one particular race with the Creator, and of other races, or of one other race, besides.

As far as the possibility of bringing forward the history of mankind as any aid to the theory of Evolution is concerned, I might have very well let the subject alone, or even noticed it more briefly than I have done. For, in truth, there is no *evidence* whatsoever, and all that the denier of creation can resort to is a supposed analogy and a probability that the peculiarities of man could be accounted for in this way or in that. But the main purpose of my brief allusion is to introduce the fact that, as far as any evidence to the contrary goes, we have an absolutely sudden appearance of man on the scene, and no kind of transitional form. Not only so, but there is no trace of any gradual development of man when he did appear. There was the first palaeolithic man; then a considerable geologic perturbation of the earth's surface, resulting in the upheaval of the cliffs in which the caves of remains occur, and in the alteration of the gravel beds in which the human remains are found; and then the neolithic age, with its evidently greater civilization (as evidenced by pottery, &c.) connected with early and traditional, but still with recent, history; but no trace of any development of one race into the other.

The absence of all progressive change is forcibly indicated by the measurements of ancient skulls, which, though not found along with the flint tools, have been found elsewhere. It has been fully shown that they differ in no respect from the skulls of men at the present day; while the skulls of the apes most nearly anthropoid, or allied to the human form, remain as widely separated in brain-capacity as ever.[1]

Thus the fact remains, that no intermediate form between the ape and the lowest man has been discovered, and that there is nothing like any progressive development in the races of man. These facts, taken together with what has been brought forward in the last chapter, show how completely the theory of the descent of man breaks down; how utterly unproved and untenable is the idea that he should have been evolved by natural causes and by slow steps from any lower form of animal life.

CHAPTER IX.

CONCLUDING REMARKS.

It will naturally be asked, "If there is all this objection to some parts of the theory of Evolution, or to that theory in an extreme or absolute form, how is it that it has been so eagerly accepted in the ranks of scientific men?"

The answer is, in the first place, because the theory of Evolution is to a great extent true. When men speak of controversy with the Evolutionist and so forth, they of course mean such as insist on carrying the doctrine to a total and even virulent denial of any Divine control at all. And it must, I think, be admitted that much of the theological opposition offered to the doctrine was aimed at *this* aspect of it. At first, men zealous for what they believed to be Divine truth, did not discriminate; they saw that the then new idea of evolution was, in many branches of its application, still very poorly proved, and they conceived that it could not be accepted apart from a total denial of religion. We have grown wiser in the course of time: misconceptions have been swept away; and everybody may be content with the assurance that there is no necessary connection even, far less any antagonism, between evolution and the Christian faith at all. We may admit all that is known of the one without denying the other.

Where the controversy has to be maintained is, that some will insist (like Professor Haeckel) in carrying evolution beyond what evidence will warrant; and not only so, but will insist on polemically putting down all religion on the strength of their improved theories. If "Evolutionists" complain of the treatment they have received at the hands of "Theologians," they will at least, in fairness, admit that there has been some misconception, some error on both sides. What we maintain is, that evolution (i.e., here, as always, unlimited, uncontrolled evolution) still fails to account for many facts in nature; that we are still far from holding anything like a complete scheme in our hands; there may be *limits* to the wide circle of progressive changes, to the results of development, of which we are ignorant; and there is, above all, in that most important of all questions - the descent of man - an absolute want of proof of animal *descent* (i.e., in any sense which includes the "soul" or spiritual faculties of man). Hence that evolution in no way clashes with an intelligent Christian belief. In saying this, I would carefully avoid undervaluing the services which the evolution theory has rendered, and is rendering, to science. Even in its first form as a mere hypothesis, it was an eminently suggestive one; there was from the first quite truth enough in it to make it fruitful, and many working hypotheses have been immensely useful in science, which have in the end been very largely modified. Before Darwin's wonderfully accurate mind and marvellous skill in collecting and making use of facts, turned the current of natural science into this new channel, men seemed to be without an aim for their naturalist's work. The *savant*, for example, procured an animal evidently of the cat tribe, and another species like a polecat. He knew as a fact that the feline teeth had a certain structure, and that the dental formula of the viverrine animals is different. Here, then, he could distinguish and perhaps name the species; but what more was to be done? All natural history as a study seemed to end in classifying and giving long names to plants and animals. The Evolution theory at once gave it a new object. Why is the dental formula of the *viverrinae* different? What purpose has the long spur in the flower of *Angraecum*, or the marvellous bucket of *Coryanthes*, the flytrap of *Dionaea*, the pitcher of *Nepenthes*? What is the cause, what is the purpose, what is the plan in the scheme of nature, of these structures? Under the stimulus of such questions naturalists woke up to new views of classification, to new experiments, inquiries, and to research for facts and the explanation of facts, in all quarters of the globe. No wonder that science rose, under such an impulse, as a butterfly from its chrysalis. But some will not be satisfied with any scheme the parts of which are separated, or which admits of anything unknown or unexplainable. They want to unite all into one grand and simple whole, which glorifies their own intelligence, and does not force them to humble patience and waiting for more light. And then the fatal enmity of the human heart - which is a plain fact, an undeniable tendency - delights to get rid of the idea of God's Sovereignty, the humbling sense that everything is at His absolute disposal, and nothing could be but as He wills it. It seems so satisfactory to eliminate all external mysterious power, to make the whole "*totus teres atque rotundus*" - having started the great machine of being *somehow* to see it all expand and unroll of itself and advance to the end.

Imagination leaps the chasms, minimizes the difficulties, passes from the possible to the certain, from the "may have been" to the "must have been" and to "it was so," and, fascinated with the *completeness* of its scheme, commences to denounce and revile as ignorant and unscientific all that would, calmly appeal to evidence, and confess ignorance, or at least a suspended judgment, in any stage where the evidence is negative or incomplete.

It has been well observed that "men are so constituted that completeness gives a special kind of satisfaction of its own, and a habit of specially regarding the general uniformity of nature begets a desire to assume its absolute and universal uniformity."

There *is* a great mystery underlying life and the plan in which the animal form, the organs of sight, hearing, and the rest, run through the whole creation: and, given a mystery, there is always ample room for speculation. Taking firm hold of the facts of development and variation, the extreme evolutionist is carried away with the idea of having the same principle throughout: he is impatient of any line or any check; he is therefore prepared to ignore all difficulties, to hope against hope for the discovery of to him necessary - but, alas, non-existent - intermediate forms, till at last he comes to deny, not only his God, but his own soul, as a spiritual and supra-physical entity.[1]

Such extremes are no part of true science, and have neither helped the progress of knowledge, nor advanced the condition of mankind. But, on the other hand, let us hear no more of a sweeping condemnation of the theory of Evolution as a whole; let us beware of any insistence on, or assumption of, the supposed fact that God created separately - ready-made and complete - all known animal forms, bringing them up from the ground, like the armed men in the Greek legend, from the dragon's teeth.

We have no more right to dogmatize and assume a scheme of creation from a popular and long-accepted interpretation of the Bible, than the evolutionist has to ignore the palpable evidences of Divine guidance and design, and construct a theory or organic being which ignores both.

PART II

CHAPTER X.

THE GENESIS NARRATIVE - ITS IMPORTANCE.

We have now completed the first portion of our inquiry: there remains the second, which, to a large class, at any rate, will appear of not less importance. For the Scriptures, which they have been taught to trust, contain a brief but direct and positive statement regarding Creation, as well as numerous other less direct allusions to the subject, all (as far as I know) in unquestioned harmony with the first.

Is the account in the Book of Genesis true? It is necessary to answer this question, because, even if a general belief in an Almighty Author and Designer of all things is shown to be reasonable, still the Scripture ought surely to support the belief; and it would be strange if, when we came to test it on this subject, we found its professed explanations would not stand being confronted with the facts.

No one will, I think, deny that the question is important. Writers of the "anti-theological" school still continue to insist on the falsity of the Mosaic narrative, as if the error was not yet sufficiently slain, and was important enough to be attacked again and again. And theological writers, down to the most modern, continue to explain the text in one way or another; - besides, *they* admit the importance, under any circumstances. I do not forget that there is a school of thought, which is distinctly Christian in its profession, but does not allow the importance. It would regard the narrative as addressed to Jews only, and therefore as one which does not concern us. If that was all, it would not be needful for me to discuss the position. But it has been held, not only that the narrative does not concern us, but *also* that it is certainly inaccurate.

This view I cannot adopt: it seems not quite fair to ourselves, and not quite fair to the Jews. Let me explain what I mean. If we have nothing to do with the narrative, let us abstain *equally* from defending it *or* pronouncing it wrong - that is for ourselves. As to the Jewish Church, a little more must be said. Let us admit, at any rate for argument's sake, that the separation between the Jewish formal and ceremonial religion and Christianity is as wide as can be wished. Nor would I undervalue the importance of insisting on pure Christianity, as distinct from Judaism. And, further, let us (without any question as to ultimate objects) regard the narrative as primarily addressed to Jews, and let us admit that it may have been unimportant, for the purpose of the first steps in Divine knowledge, that any account should be given of Creation beyond the primary fact that all idolatrous cosmogonies were false, and that the Unseen God of Israel alone made the heavens and the earth "in the beginning." Why should the Jews have received that truth through the medium of a story of which the whole framework was false, and nothing but the moral true? The framework, moreover, is one so plainly *professing to be fact*, that it was certain to be received as such by a simple people. It seems to me that there is something very suspicious, something repugnant to notions of truth and honest dealing, in the possible communication of underlying Divine truth through the medium of stories, which are not stories on the face of them, but profess and pretend to be statements of fact and authoritatively made.

But, further, it cannot be denied that, whatever allowance may have to be made under the early Jewish dispensation for the ideas and weaknesses of a semi-barbarous people, whatever "winking" there may have been "at times of ignorance," the main object was, by a gradual revelation,[1] by a system of typical ordinances and ceremonies, to lead up to the full spiritual light of the Christian dispensation. Everything written, said, or done, was a step - however small an one - always tending in the one direction, according to the usual law of Evolution. The Christian believer may then look back to the early stages as imperfect foreshadowings and dim illustrations of the whole truth; but he would, I should think, on any ordinary principles, be shocked to find truth developed out of positive error. And should the error have been discovered, as it now is[2] (in the view of these I am contending against), this discovery might have arrested the further development of Divine truth altogether. If Moses, or whoever wrote the Book of Genesis - we will not cavil at that - was allowed to compose his own fancies or beliefs on the subject of Creation, *and to state them as Divine fact* (no matter that the reader at the time was not able to find out the error), would not grave suspicion attach to whatever else he put forward? Who could tell that, on any other subject, the plainest and most direct statement of fact was not equally a fancy, only embodying or enshrining (under the guise of its errors) some real Divine facts? If Genesis i. is unreliable, we have a case of a writer going out of his way to add to certain truths, which might easily have been stated by themselves, a number of positive declarations, *as of Divine authority*, regarding facts, which are not facts.

The great truths that God is really the Maker and Author of all things, and that man has a spiritual being, and so forth, surely *gain nothing* from being conveyed to the world in the folds of a fable. And when it is not in a confessed fable, but a fable put forth as fact - "God said," "God created," "it was so" - not only is there no gain, but our sense of fitness and of truth receive a shock. A parable is always discernible as a parable, a vision as a vision. When our Lord, for example, tells us of the ten virgins, we do not suppose Him to be revealing the actual existence of ten such maidens, wise and foolish. We know that He is reading a lesson of watchfulness. But looking at the Genesis narrative, who could suppose it to be a parable? If sober, unmistakable statement of fact is possible, we surely have it here, in intention, at least.

The plan of teaching truth in an envelope of error is *per se* difficult to conceive. But how much worse is it when we consider - what criterion does mankind possess for disinterring and distinguishing the elements of truth? If in religion we had only to do (as some would perhaps contend) with obvious enforcements of common morality and kindness, there might be a possibility of getting over the difficulty, because man would possess some kind of criterion whereby to distinguish what was fictitious, by the simple process of considering whether any given statement bore on morals or not. Such a test would not indeed go very far, because the human race is by no means agreed on all moral questions; nor does it always find it easy to say what is, and what is not, directly or indirectly connected with morals. But, in fact, the scope of religion cannot be so confined: and then the difficulty returns; for a revelation that tells us anything of the nature of God and His method of government, of the nature of our own being and of a future state, must necessarily go beyond our own ethical knowledge and powers of judging, or it would not be a revelation. Supposing that the revelation regarding such vital subjects is occasionally conveyed through the medium of erroneous statements, where in any given case would be the certainty as to what was Divine truth, and what not so?

This argument applies equally to another school of thinkers, who do not care to tell us what the narrative in itself means: who believe that God did not do what He is said to have done in Genesis, and yet who hold that the narrative is in a sense inspired, and that we may learn from it the great facts that God (and none other) originated all things - that man has a spiritual element in his nature, and that woman is equal in nature, but subordinate in position, to man, and so forth. Not only is enlightened judgment, even, inadequate to pronounce with certainty on how much is true; but the strange feeling still remains, if God designed to teach us these truths only, why was it not possible to enable the writer[1] to state them without the (purely gratuitous) error? The sufferance of such a strange and unnecessary mixture of error seems rather like that "putting to confusion" of the human mind, which we feel sure the Great Teacher would never willingly perpetrate.

Nor, again, can the narrative be got over by saying it is a poetic side or aspect of the facts, and not to be taken literally. If any one knows exactly what this means, and can tell us always how to translate the matter into plain language, it is to be wished that he would enlighten the world as to the process. But even if such process exists infallibly and universally, still, one would suppose, the narrative must, to begin with, be unmistakable poetry. And here, again, the narrative bears every mark of an intention to state facts, not poetic aspects of facts. Nor can we take the narrative as belonging to a familiar class in Scripture where a dream is used as a vehicle of communication. In those cases there is really no room for doubt; the visible facts themselves are obviously designed only to typify or represent some other facts.

The events stated in Genesis are not of this class. Those, therefore, who would be content with getting over the narrative without caring for its details, can, I must suspect, have hardly given adequate attention to the form and to the contents of the narrative as it stands. Not only are the statements positive, but, taking any interpretation whatever of them, they are not nearly imaginative enough to suit the purpose.

They have an obvious amount of relation to fact which has never been denied.[1]

If the narrative is purely human even (and that the school we are considering do not aver), how did the writer come to be accurate even to that extent? Take only the order of events. I admit it does not correspond with the geologic record in the way commonly asserted; yet it has a very remarkable relation to that sequence.

Now, in any case, the writer could have had no knowledge of any kind *of his own* on the subject: how did he hit on this particular arrangement?[2] It is a mere matter of calculation on the well-known rules of permutation and combination to realize in how many different ways the same set of events could have been arranged; the number is very considerable.

And he could derive no assistance from any similar existing narrative. If we conclude from the Assyrian discoveries that a non-biblical but similar narrative existed, still it is certain that the principal one we as yet have is so late in date, that it is more likely to be derived from the Bible than the Bible from it. And though, on referring to the earlier tablets, we find traces of the same narrative, it is so obscured by idolatrous and false details, that the Bible writer must have had to make a virtually new departure to get his own simple narrative. A re-revelation would be required. As to all other cosmogonies, Egyptian, Indian, and Buddhistic, nothing can be more opposed in principle and in detail than they are to the severe and stately simplicity and directness of the Mosaic.

We cannot, then, account for the narrative on human grounds; nor can we suppose that any inspiring control would have given the author so much truth, and yet allowed so much error.

All this points to only one of two possible conclusions: either the narrative is not inspired at all, and is a mere misleading story, into which the name of God is introduced by the author's piety - and so really teaches us nothing, since it is not revelation; *or* the narrative is, as a whole, divinely dictated, and must be true *throughout*, if we can only arrive by due study at its true meaning. That part of it is, or may be, true, even on the most cursory study, is not denied; that it is *all* true will appear, I think, in the sequel.

But there is a shorter and simpler reason why the rejection of the narrative in Genesis would be a direct blow to Christian faith. The plain truth is that it can hardly be denied, by any candid student of the New Testament, that our Lord and His apostles certainly received the early chapters of Genesis as of Divine authority. This has always been perceived by the whole school of writers opposed to the Faith. They therefore continue to attack these early revelations, and rejoice to overturn them if they can, because they are aware that hardly any chapters in the Bible are more constantly alluded to and made the foundation of practical arguments by our Lord and His apostles.

If these chapters can be shown to be mythical, then the Divine knowledge of our Lord as the Son of God, and the inspiration of His apostles, are called in question. In the New Testament, especially, there are repeated and striking allusions to Adam, the temptation of the woman by the Serpent, and the entrance into the world of sin and death. Our Lord Himself places the whole argument of His teaching on marriage and the permissibility of divorce on Genesis ii. 24 (*cf.* St. Matt. xix. And St. Mark x.). In St. John viii. 44 our Lord clearly alludes to the Edenic narrative when He speaks of the tempter as a "manslayer ([Greek: anthropoktonos]) from the beginning." Still more remarkable is the argument of St. Paul in Romans v.; altogether based as it is on the historical verity of the account of the Fall; and other allusions are to be found in 1 Cor. xi. 8, in 2 Cor. xi. 3, in the Epistle to the Ephesians, and elsewhere. In short, there are at least sixty-six passages in the New Testament, in which the first eleven chapters of Genesis are directly quoted or made the ground of argument. Of these, six are by our Lord Himself, two being direct quotations;[1] six by St. Peter, thirty-eight by St. Paul, seven by St. John, one by St. James, two by St. Jude, two by the assembled apostles, three by St. Luke, and one by St. Stephen.

We cannot, in fact, possibly avoid the conclusion that our Lord and His apostles admitted the Divine origin and historical truth of these chapters.

Therefore, we are bound as Christians to accept them, and that without glossing or frittering away their meaning, when we have arrived, by just processes, at what that meaning really is.

The fact just stated further warns us against accepting an indefinite interpretation which, while it acknowledges the truth of the general conclusion, still virtually, if not in so many words, allows that the details may be wholly inaccurate.

CHAPTER XI.

SCRIPTURE METHODS OF REVELATION.

Passing, then, to a consideration of the explanations of the narrative that may be or have been given at various times, I would first call attention to the fact, that it seems in many instances to have been the distinct purpose of Divine inspiration to allow the meaning of some passages to be obscure; perhaps among other reasons, that men might be compelled to study closely, to reason and to compare, and thus to become more minutely acquainted with the record. Especially in a case of this sort, where the world's knowledge of the facts would necessarily be gradual, was it desirable that the narrative should be confined in scope, and capable of being worked out and explained by the light of later discoveries; because, had the narrative really (as has long been supposed) been revealed to tell us what was the actual course of evolution of created forms on earth, it would not only have occupied a disproportionate space in the sacred volume, but would have been unintelligible to the world for many centuries, and would have given rise to much doubting and false argument, to the great detriment of men's spiritual enlightenment. It would have diverted men's minds from the great moral and conclusion of the whole (and here it is that the "moral" or conclusion is so important) to set them arguing on points of natural science.

The Bible was never intended (so far we may agree with all the schools of thought) to be a text-book on biology or geology. We need rather to be impressed with the great facts of God's Sovereignty and Providence, and to know definitely that all the arrangements of our globe and all forms of life are due to Divinely-created types. This is exactly secured by the narrative as it stands; but such a purpose would not be served by a narrative which, while it contained these great facts, had them enwrapped in a tissue of unnecessary and false details. And therefore it is, if I may so far anticipate my conclusion, that the narrative has no direct concern with how, when, and where, the Creation slowly worked itself out under the Divine guidance which is still elaborating the great purpose of the "ages"; it confines our attention to what God, the great Designer, did and said in heaven, as preliminary to all that was to follow on earth. The former was not a proper subject for revelation, because man would in time come to learn it by his studies on earth; but the latter all ages could only learn - the first as well as the latest - from a Divine Revelation.

Again, let me address a few words to those who are tempted, half unconsciously perhaps, to think that any lengthy prelude and "elaborate" explanation of Genesis must condemn the narrative *a priori*, or be derogatory to the dignity of Revelation. Why the narrative should be brief and concise I have just suggested. That it needs explanation of *some* sort is inevitable, because it *must* be put into human language; and directly such language is employed, we come upon such terms as "let there be," "he created," and "days," which do not always call forth the same ideas in all minds.

It will not have escaped the attention of any earnest student, that Scripture has several different methods of describing things so as to reveal them to men. This, a moment's reflection will enable us to expect. However high and wonderful the things to be stated are, in order to be brought within reach of human understanding *they must be expressed in terms of human thought and experience*; and these are imperfect and essentially inadequate. Hence it is, that many truths have to be brought before us in special or peculiar ways.

How, for instance, are we told of the temptation and fall of man? How are we to understand what was meant by the Tree of Life or the Tree of Knowledge of Good and Evil, or by the Serpent speaking and beguiling Eve? We are at a great loss to give a precise explanation, though the practical meaning is not difficult.

The facts may be none the less true, though from their transcendental character it may have been necessary to put them down in mysterious, possibly even in merely allegorical, language. Another instance of this might be given in the account of Satan in the presence of the Lord as described in the Book of Job, or of the lying Spirit described by Micaiah when prophesying before Ahab. It maybe that these narratives describe to us transactions in a world beyond our own, which *could* only be conveyed to us in figures or in imperfect form. When St. Paul was caught up into the third heaven, he "heard unspeakable things" which it was not *possible* for him to utter - the medium of expression was wanting. Divine or mysterious things have, then, to be described in peculiar language which is not always easy to understand. Nor, having respect to the varying requirements of the different ages, or the circumstances of the time and of the inspired writer, is it easy to understand why any particular form of communication was selected, though doubtless if we knew more we should see a good reason for it. This gives us one class of Scripture passages - of methods of revelation. On the other hand, there are in Scripture many facts of the highest import, and in themselves of transcendent magnitude, which are yet capable of being stated without any possibility of our interpreting or understanding the narrative in more ways than one. When it is stated that Christ Jesus rose from the dead, we know beyond all reasonable doubt what is meant. The fact may be true or false, but the narrative of the fact needs no explanation; there are no terms which need expansion - which could bear more than one possible meaning, and which could be used accordingly in one sense or another. This instances a second class. Again, we can bring forward yet another class of Scripture revelations, namely, passages which are necessarily understood with reference to certain other matters which are unexpressed but are taken for granted, or in which the words used may bear more than one meaning, or a meaning which is uncertain or obscure. If the unexpressed matter can be supplied without doubt, then all ages will agree in the interpretation; and if the terms can (by reference to context or otherwise) be explained, the same result follows: if not, then in interpreting the narrative, each age will *make its own assumption* regarding the terms used, on the basis of such knowledge as it possesses. It follows, then, inevitably, that if the state of knowledge varies, the interpretation will be different according to the different standard of knowledge, according to which the necessary assumptions are made. And yet all the while the authority of the passage itself is not touched. As it is unquestionable that such different classes of passage do occur in Scripture, it is merely a question of criticism whether any given passage is of this class or that, and whether its terms do admit of or require explanation. It is no doubt possible to make mistakes and to err by refusing the direct meaning, and giving to the terms an assumed meaning for which there is no real necessity.[1] We have always to be on our guard against giving special meanings to words where they are not required; but granted that caution, there undoubtedly are passages in which either the terms themselves are not plain, or in which they may really have a meaning different from the ordinary one.

To descend from the general to the particular, it is obvious that the account of Creation in Genesis i., ii. is in such a form that we must assume our own ideas of the term "day" therein employed, and also those to be attached to "created" and similar terms.

In early times, no one would take "day" to mean anything else but an earth day of the ordinary kind, and no one would question whether or not the whole existing animals and plants, or their ancestors, appeared on earth in six such days, or whether anything else was meant. Again, by the time St. Augustine was writing, a little more knowledge of nature and a little more habit of reasoning about the origin of things was in the world, and that knowledge led people to suppose that creation meant only the making of things "out of nothing," but that it would take longer than six times twelve hours, so that "days" might mean "periods."

And people imagined for a long time that - taking for an example the work in the middle of the narrative - there was a time when the earth emerged from the tumult of waters, that it then got covered with plants, the waters remaining barren of life; but that when the plants had come up all over the ground, then the waters all at once became full of all sorts of sea-shells, fish, and monsters of the deep, and so on.

They did all this, by naturally *assuming* that the terms "creation," "day," &c., meant what the *existing state of knowledge* at the time suggested.

At the present day, one would have supposed that every one must feel that while the term "day" might or might not admit of explanation, certainly *creation* (i.e., terms implying it) did require very great care in interpreting, and very great consideration as to what they really meant But however that may be, we have here a passage which *must* have an explanation; and which must have an explanation that depends on the state of knowledge.

The utility of Revelation is not negatived by this necessary result of the employment of human language in describing the facts. It was *not* necessary before, that all should be understood; it may be now increasingly necessary in the purposes of God that it should be. At any rate the fact is so, that in former days people did not possess the data for knowing fully what creation meant, and certainly they do now possess it to a very much greater extent at least. Always men could learn from the narrative what it always was important for them to learn, namely, God's Sovereignty and Authorship. It is in this way that the value of the *general* teaching of the narrative comes out, and not by trying to allow a mixture of truth and falsehood in Revelation. All is and always was true; but *all* the truth was not equally extractable at all times.

Again: the dignity of the old written Revelation is not compromised because God has virtually given a further revelation in His works, i.e., by enabling man to know more about the rock-strata and the succession of life on the earth. That is what it really comes to. It should never be forgotten that the book of Nature *is* a revelation.

The *works* of God, if interpreted truly, are evidence of the same nature as the *word* of God if interpreted truly. God has created man and his reason. It is impossible to suppose that it can be unrighteous reasoning in God's sight, to derive from the facts of nature any legitimate conclusion to which those facts point. It is childish to believe that God created ready-made - if I may so speak - rocks with fossils in them, marks of rain-drops showing which way the wind blew at the time, footprints of birds, animals with remains of the prey they had been feeding on, in their stomachs, and so forth. It is perfectly reasonable and right to conclude certainly, that those creatures were once living beings; that the surface of the earth was once a soft sediment which received the impression of the rain-drops as they fell; and that stratified rocks were deposited out of lakes and seas, as we see alluvial strata deposited at the present day. It is impossible, therefore, that (if we are not misled by appearances) any well-ascertained fact can be contrary to the truth of God as explained by Revelation. If we are not sure of the facts of nature, we must wait patiently till further knowledge enlightens us, and must not hastily conclude that the Bible is wrong. The repeated corrections which successive years have compelled us to make in conclusions which were once firmly accepted and proclaimed as "truths of science," should teach us caution in this respect.

Nor, lastly, is it any reproach to the Church, as keeper of the Divine Revelation, that its opinion of certain passages should vary with the growth of knowledge. It would be hardly necessary to make this obvious remark but for the fact that it has been reproached against Christian belief, that science is contrary to the Bible, and that the Church has ever had to confess itself wrong, after having persecuted people for not following its peculiar views. It is, indeed, unfortunate that a blind zeal for God has led, in the past, to persecution; the Church failing to see that such men as Galileo and Bruno never denied God at all, nor did their discoveries really contradict the Word. But persecution is not a sin peculiar to the Church; it is a sin of human nature.

It is also true that Christian views may be wrong, but the fault is in the views, not in the Bible.

Scientific men, of all people, should be the last to complain of *change* in views, seeing that what was science two hundred years ago is now (much of it) exploded nonsense.

There is no harm whatever in changing our views about the meaning of difficult passages - provided we never let go our hold on the central truth, and put the error to our own account, not saying that the Word itself is wrong.

It may, in this connection, be at once observed that any particular explanation, or that one which I propose presently to suggest, of the first chapters of Genesis, may not commend itself to the reader, and yet the general argument I have adduced will hold good notwithstanding.

All that I care to contend is, that science does not contradict a syllable of the narrative on *one* possible interpretation, and that changes in view as to interpretation are no arguments against the truth of the passage itself.

CHAPTER XII.

METHODS OF INTERPRETING THE NARRATIVE - ASSUMPTIONS OF MEANING TO CERTAIN TERMS.

Returning, then, to the narrative in the Book of Genesis, I think we may take it as clear that the passage stands in such a concise and condensed form, that it is obviously open to *be interpreted*. Further, that we should not be surprised if the interpretation at the present day, with our vastly increased knowledge of Nature, is different from what it was in earlier times.

I make no apology for repeating this so often, because it is really amazing to see the way in which "anti-theological" writers attack what *they suppose* to be the interpretation of the narrative, or what some one else supposes to be such, and seem to be satisfied that in so doing they have demolished the credibility of the narrative itself.

If you choose to assume that Creation as spoken of by the sacred writer means some particular thing, or even if the mass of uneducated or unreflecting people assume it and you follow them, I grant at once that the narrative can be readily made out to be wrong.

Permit me, then, to repeat once more, that the narrative

is in human language, and uses the human terms "created," "made," and "formed," and that these terms *do* (as a matter of fact which there is no gainsaying) bear a meaning which is not invariable. Hence, without any glossing or "torturing" of the narrative, we are under the plain obligation to seek to assign to these terms a true meaning *with all the light that modern knowledge* can afford.

Now (having already considered the school of interpretation which declines to attend to the exact terms) we can confine our attention to two classes of interpreters. One explains the term "days" to mean long periods of time; the other accepts the word in its ordinary and most natural sense, and endeavours to eliminate the long course of developmental work made known to us by palaeontological science, and supposes all that to have been passed over in silence; and argues that a final preparation for the advent of the man Adam was made in a special work of six days.

All the well-known attempts at explanation, such as those of Pye-Smith, Chalmers, H. Miller, Pratt, and the ordinary commentaries, can be placed in one or other of these categories.

Now, as regards both, I recur to the curious fact (already noted) that it seems never to enter into the conception of either school to inquire for a moment what the sacred writer meant by "created" - God "created" - God said "let there be." It *is* curious, because no one can reasonably say "these terms are obvious, they bear their own meaning on the surface;" a moment's analysis will scatter such an idea to the winds. Yet the terms *are* passed by. The commentators set themselves right earnestly to compare and to collate, to argue and to analogize, on the meaning of the term "days;" the other term "created" they take for granted without - as far as I am aware - single line of explanation, or so much as a doubt whether they know what it really means!

The interpretation that I would propose to the judgment of the Church is just the very opposite. It seems to me that the word *day* as used in the narrative needs no explanation; it seems to me that the other does. As regards the term "day," it is surely a rule of sound criticism never to give an "extraordinary" meaning to a word, when the "ordinary" one will give good and intelligible sense to a passage. And looking to the fact that, after all, when the days of Genesis *are* explained to mean periods of very unequal but possibly enormous duration, that explanation is not only quite useless, but raises greater difficulties than ever, I should think it most likely that the "day" of the narrative should be taken in the ordinary sense. But of this hereafter.

On the other hand, with regard to the terms "creation,[1]" "created," "Let there be," and so forth, I find ample room for the most careful consideration and for detailed study before we can say what is meant. Even then there remains a feeling of profound mystery. For at the very beginning of every train of reflection and reasoning on the subject, we are just brought up dead at this wonderful fact, the existence of *matter* where previously there had been *nothing*. The phrase "created *out of* nothing" is of course a purely conventional one, and, strictly speaking, has no meaning; but we adopt it usefully enough to indicate our ultimate fact - the appearance of matter where previously there had been nothing. Nor is the difficulty really surmounted by alleging such a mere *phrase* as "matter is eternal," for we have just as little mental conception of self-existent, always - and *without beginning* - existent matter, as we have of "creation out of nothing."

The human mind has always a difficulty when it is brought face to face with something that is beyond the scope not only of its own practical, but, even of its theoretical or potential ability.

The "creation," therefore, of matter by a Divine Power is matter of *faith*, as I endeavoured to set forth in the earlier pages of this little work; but it is *reasonable* faith, because it can be supported by sound reasoning from analogy and strong probability.

All our attention, then, I submit, should be directed to understanding what is "creation" in the sacred narrative.

CHAPTER XIII.

THE GENESIS NARRATIVE CONSIDERED GENERALLY.

I. - THE FIRST PART OF THE NARRATIVE.

Sec. 1. *Objections to the Received Interpretations.*

Taking the narrative as it stands, we find it to consist of two parts. First, a general statement, of which no division of time is predicated, and which is unaccompanied by any detail. Second, there is an account seriatim of certain operations which are stated to have been severally performed one on each of six days.

As regards the first portion, we have no definite knowledge of scientific truth with which to compare the narrative. It is obviously necessary for some Divine teacher to tell us authoritatively that God originated and caused the material earth, and the systems of suns and stars which men on the earth's surface are able to discern in the "heavens."

We are consequently informed that in the beginning - there is no practical need for defining further - "God created the heavens and the earth." Here the question arises whether the Hebrew "bara," which is a general term, alludes to the first production of material, or to the moulding or fashioning of material already (in terms) assumed to exist. I think that the conclusion must be that the best authority is in favour of the idea of absolute origination of the whole; - the bringing the entire system into existence where previously there was a perfect blank. But even if the secondary meaning of "fashioned" or "forged" be allowed, we have still an intelligible rendering. For in that case the first origination of matter is tacitly assumed by the term itself, and the statement would be, that the matter of the future cosmos so existing, the Divine Artificer fashioned or moulded it into the orderly fabric it has come to be.

The narrative then at once refers to our earth, with which, and with its inhabitants, the whole volume is to be in future directly concerned. "The earth was (or became) without form and void (chaotic), and darkness was on the face of the deep (or abyss)."

We have no positive knowledge of what the first condition of terrestrial matter was, apart from Revelation. The remarkable discoveries that the spectroscope has enabled, and the facts learned from the physical history of comets and meteorites, can do no more than make what is known as the "nebular hypothesis" highly probable. But it is amply sufficient for our purpose to point out, that if it is true that matter originated in a nebulous haze to the particles of which a spiral rotatory motion had been communicated, and if (confining our attention to one planet only) that attenuated matter gradually aggregated in a ring or rings, and then consolidated into a solid or partly solid globe, then the results are briefly, but adequately and sublimely, provided for by the form of the

Mosaic statement.

Matter thus aggregating would have developed an enormous amount of heat, and there would have been a seething mass of molten mineral matters, with gases and other materials in the form of vapours, which would have gradually cooled and consolidated. Vast masses of water would in time be formed on one hand, and solid mineral masses on the other; the latter would contract as cooling progressed, causing great upheavals and depressions and contortions of strata. And before the advent of life-forms, it is not difficult to conceive that the first state of our globe was one which is intelligibly and very graphically described as being "without form and void." Nothing more than that, can, from actual physical knowledge, be stated.[1]

It is also stated that this confused elemental state of our earth was accompanied at first by darkness. Material darkness that is - for the potentiality of light and order was there; the SPIRIT OF GOD "moved" (or brooded) upon the face of the abyss. This presents no difficulty of interpretation, and may therefore be passed over for the present.

Practically, indeed, there has been no grave difficulty raised over this first portion. And if it is argued (on the ground of what I have already in general terms indicated) that the term "created" will, on my own interpretation, get us into difficulties, I reply that here, in its position and with the context, there is no room for doubt, for clearly the word implies *both* the great primary idea of the Divine design or plan formulated in heaven, *and* the subsequent result in time and space.[1] This will become more clear when I have further explained the subject.

II. - THE SECOND PART OF THE NARRATIVE.

But from this point the narrative commences to be more precise, and to exhibit a very singular and altogether unprecedented division of creative work into "days."

Now I have already indicated my doubt whether we ought to import any unusual meaning to explain this term.

In the first place, the objection that till the movements and relations of the sun to the earth were ordained there would be no *measure of a day* will not stand a moment's examination. Nor will the further objection sometimes made, that even with the sun, a day is a very uncertain thing: for example, a day and a night in the north polar regions are periods of month-long duration, quite different from what they are in England, or at Mount Sinai. Obviously, a "day" with reference to the planet for which the term is used, means the period occupied by one rotation of the planet on its own axis. The rotation of the earth is antecedent to anything mentioned in the narrative we are considering. In the nature of things, it would have been coeval with the introduction of the *prima materies* - at least if any nebular hypothesis can be relied on. The "day" would be there whether it were obscured by vapours or not, and whether specially made countable and recognizable by what we call the rising and setting of the sun, or not, and whether we were standing in Nova Zembla or in Australia.

Nor is it of much use to refer to the general use of "day" for indefinite periods, which is just as common in the English of to-day as it was in the Hebrew of the Old Testament. But the double use of the term in different senses has become general, just because it was found in practice that no confusion ordinarily resulted; and surely such a practice would not have been common, or at any rate would have been specially avoided in the sacred volume, wherever any mistake or confusion was likely or even possible.

No one can mistake what is meant when allusion is made to "the day in which God made the heaven and the earth." No one falls into doubt when the "days" of the prophets are spoken of - any more than they do now when a man says, "Such a thing will not happen in my *day*."

Whenever in Daniel, or in similar prophetic writings, the term "day" is used in a peculiar sense as indicating a term of years, we have no difficulty in recognizing the fact from the context and circumstances of the narrative; nor am I aware that any controversy has ever arisen regarding the use of the term "day" *in any passage of Scripture excepting in this.*

This fact alone is suspicious; the more so, because there is absolutely nothing in the context to indicate that anything but an ordinary day is intended. Not only so, but there *is* in the context something that does very clearly indicate (and I think Dr. Reville is perfectly justified in insisting on this) that an ordinary terrestrial day is meant. One of the primeval institutions of Divine Providence for men, my readers will not need to be reminded, was that of a "Sabbath," which any one reading the text would understand to mean a day, and which the Jews - the earliest formal or legal recognizers of it - *did* so understand, and that under direct Divine sanction.

If the *days* of Genesis mean indefinite periods of aeonian duration, how is the seventh *day* of rest to be understood?

But even if these difficulties are overcome, absolutely nothing is gained by taking the day to be a period.

I presume that the object of gaining long periods of time instead of days in reading the Mosaic record, is to assume that the narrative means to describe the actual production on the earth of all that was created; in other words, to assume a particular meaning for the words "created," "brought forth," &c and then to make out that if a whole age is granted, Science will allow us a sequence of a "plant age" a "fish and saurian age," a "bird age," and a "mammalian age"; - that is, in general terms and neglecting minor forms of life. But then *to make any sense at all with the verses* we are bound to show that each age preceded the next - that one was more than partly, if not quite completely, established *before* any appearance of the next.

It is to this interpretation that Professor Huxley alludes when he says, in his first article,[1] "There must be some position from which the reconcilers of Science and Genesis will not retreat - some central idea the maintenance of which is vital , and its refutation fatal.... It is that the animal species which compose the water population, the air population, and the land population,[2] respectively, originated during three successive periods of time, and only during those periods of time."

For my own part, I hasten to say that, as one of the

despised race of "reconcilers," not only is this idea no central position from which I will not retreat, but one which I should never think of occupying for one moment.

But on the view of the *periods*, some such position must be taken up. And if so, I must maintain that Professor Huxley has shown - if indeed it was not obvious already - that the idea of a series of periods, and in each of which a certain kind of life began and culminated (if it was not fully completed) *before* another began, is untrue to nature. This, therefore, cannot have been intended by the author of Genesis.

I will here interrupt my argument for a moment to say that there is a *certain degree* of *coincidence* between the succession of life on the earth as far as it is explained by palaeontological research, and the order of creation stated in Genesis; but that is not concerned with any forced interpretation of the term "day." The coincidence is just near enough to give rise to a desire to identify creative periods with the series shown by the fossil-bearing rocks; while it is attended with just enough of difference to furnish matter for controversy, and to expose the interpreters to be cut up.

But to return. Nothing, I submit, is gained by getting *day* to mean period. Let us put the matter quite squarely. Let us take day to mean period, and let us take all the verses to mean the *process* of *producing* on earth the various life-forms.

In order to come at once to the point, let us begin with the time when the dry land and the waters are separate. At that moment, there is nothing said (or implied) about life already having begun in either water or on dry land. God commanded plants to grow; consequently during that *whole period* nothing but plants, and that of all the kinds and classes mentioned, should appear either in water or on land. That period being done, then came the command for water animals, fish and great monsters, and also birds. We ought, accordingly, to come next upon a whole period in which no trace of anything but plants and these animals can be found; and lastly, we ought to find the period of mammalia, smaller reptiles, *amphibia* and insects (creeping things).

That is the fair and plain result of what comes of supposing the terms "let there be," &c., to mean *production on earth of the thing's themselves*, and that the days are long *periods*.

All overlapping of the periods is inadmissible. All meaning is taken away, if we allow of fish (e.g.) appearing in the middle of our first period; for God did not command another day's work till after the first was completed - "there was evening and there was morning, a first day" (period), &c.

No; to suit the text so interpreted, we must have a full *period* of plants with no fish; then a period of both but no insects, no creeping things, no animals; and so on. Now it is quite idle to contend any longer, that any such state of things ever existed.

If we pass over the long series of the most ancient strata in which doubtful forms of obscure elementary plant and animal life appear *almost* together, we shall come to shell-fish, and crustaceans fully established in the water, and scorpions, and some insects even on land, *before* plants made any great show. For the

Carboniferous - *the* age of acrogen plants, *par excellence* - does not occur till after swarms of *Trilobite* Crustaceans had filled the sea and passed away, and after the Devonian fish-age had nearly passed away; and so on throughout.

The groups in nature overlap each other so closely, that though plant-life (in elementary forms) probably had the actual start; virtually the two kingdoms - plant and animal - appeared almost simultaneously. There is nothing like the appearance of a first period in which one *alone* predominated. And long before the plants are established in all classes, the great reptiles, birds, and some mammals, had appeared. The seed-bearing plants - true grasses and exogens with seed capsules (angiosperms) did not appear till quite Tertiary times. That is the essential difference between the facts and the theory. If we make a diagram, and let the squares represent the main groups, the order (according to the period interpretation) ought to be as in A, whereas it really more resembles B. Thus.

But then it will be asked, if the day means only an ordinary day - not a long period - what is there that actually could have happened, and did happen, in *three days* (for that is the real point, as we shall see), such as the writer describes as the third, fifth, and sixth days?

I answer that on those days, and on the previous ones, God did exactly what He is recorded to have done. After the creation of light (first day), and the ideal adjustment of the distribution of land and water (second day), He (*a*) "*created*," on the third day, plants, from the lowest cryptogam upwards; then (*b*) paused for a day (the fourth) in the direct work of creating life-forms, to adjust certain matters regarding times and seasons, and regulation of climate, which doubtless would not be essential during the early stages of life evolution, but would become so directly a certain point was reached; then (*c*) resumed the direct creating work (fifth day), with fishes, great reptiles,[1] and birds (grouped purposely so, as we shall see); and, lastly (*d*), before the Day of Rest, created the group of mammals (*carnivora* and *herbivora*), the "creeping things" of the earth, and man (also grouped together).

But some one will ask, You then accept the earlier theory, that the whole life-series that is now revealed to us by the rocks, from the Laurentian to the Recent, is excluded from the narrative; and that some special acts of creation, regarding only modern and surviving life-forms, were made immediately before man appeared? By no-means; for such a theory is not only in itself improbable, but is contrary to all the evidence we possess of life-history on the earth, and is so hopeless that it is really not worth serious examination and refutation.

We have no evidence of any such gap - such sudden change in the history of life. Nor is it possible to find any place in the Mosaic story at which we could reasonably interpolate a *long* period, such as that indicated by the entire series of rock strata. For a great part of such a period, not only must there have been a regular succession of life just the same in nature (though specifically different) as that now on earth, but a regular distribution of land and water, and a settled action of the sun and the seasons, would be required. No; we must give up all the older methods which try to ignore the study of the word "created," or to assume for it a meaning that it is not intended to bear.

All depends, then, on what is meant by such terms as "created," "let there be," "let the earth bring forth," &c. Perhaps it has occurred to but few of my readers seriously to examine into their own mental conception of an "act of creation." Some will readily answer, "Of course it means only that at the Divine *fiat*, any given species - say an elephant - appeared perfect, trunk, tusks, and all the peculiar development of skull and skeleton, where previously no such creature had existed." But what possible reason have they for this conclusion? None whatever. It has simply been carelessly assumed from age to age, because people at first knew no better; and when they began to know better, they did not stop to amend their ideas accordingly.

Of course, as Professor Huxley puts it, millions of pious Jews and Christians[1] supposed *creation* to mean a "sudden act of the Deity" - i.e., to mean just what the knowledge of the time enabled them to imagine. They could do nothing else. The state of knowledge fifty years ago would not have rendered it possible for an article like Professor Huxley's (that to which allusion has several times been made) to have been written at all. What wonder, then, that the multitude did not understand what *creation* meant, and that a reasonable interpretation of the word has only become possible in quite recent times? Surely all that is the fault of the reader, not of the text. I do not even care that the writer himself did not fully apprehend the subject. When a human prophet is entrusted with the divulgation of high and wonderful things, it is quite possible that he may have been to greater or less extent in the dark as to all or some of the communication he was writing.

All that can be reasonably required is that the narrative, as it stands, shall be consistent with actual truth, and shall at no time come to be provably at variance with it.

But let us look at the word "creation" more closely. We accept what we are told, that in the beginning God called into existence force and matter, the material or "physical basis," and all other necessaries of life. Suppose, then (even dropping the question of Evolution, in order to satisfy the "pious millions"), that this "matter" was all ready (if I may so speak) to spring into organized form and being to take shape on earth - what shape should it take? Why (e.g.) an elephant? Why not any other animal, or a nondescript - a form which no zoologist could place, recognize, or classify? The *form*, the ideal structure, the *formula*, of the genus elephant must somehow have come into existence *before* the obedient materials and the suitable forces of nature could work themselves together to the desired end.

Mr. Mivart has defined "creation" at page 290 of his "Genesis of Species." There is original creation, derivative or secondary creation (where the present form has descended from an ancestor that was originally "directly" created), and conventional creation (as when a man "creates a fortune," meaning that he produces a complex state or arrangement out of simpler materials). That is perfectly true, so far; but it is only a verbal definition, and still does not go inside, into the *idea* involved. We must go farther.

In every act of creation, two requisites can clearly be distinguished: (1) the matter of life, and the forces, affinities, and local surroundings necessary; and (2) the type, plan, ideal, or formula, to realize or produce which, the forces and the matter are to act and react. This second is all-essential; without it the first would only produce a limbo of

> "Unaccomplisht works of Nature's hand,
> Abortive, monstrous, or unkindly mixt.[1]"

No *creation* in *any* sense whatever could come out of it.

In the same way, when we speak of the Divine Artificer "creating," or saying "Let there be," there are two things implied: (i) the Divine plan or type-form, and its utterance or delivery (so to speak) to the builder-forces and materials; (2) the result or the translation into tangible existence of the Divine plan.

In every passage speaking of creation it *possible* that both processes may be implied; it may be clear from the text (as in Genesis i. 1) that this is so. But it is equally possible that the first point only, which in some aspects is really the essential matter, is alone spoken of.

And I submit that, given the general fact that God originated everything in heaven and earth (as first of all stated generally in Genesis i. 1-3), the essential part of the *detailed* or *specific* creation subsequently spoken of, was the Divine origination of the types, the ideal forms, into which matter endowed with life was to develop; *without* any *necessary* reference to how, or in what time, the Divine creation was actually realized or accomplished on earth. It may be that the *form* so conceived and drawn in Nature's book by the Divine Designer is a final form, up to which development shall lead, and beyond which (at least in a material sense) it shall not go; or it may be that it is a type intended to be transitory;[1] but *both the intermediate and final forms must take their origin first in the Divine Mind, and be prescribed from the Heavenly Throne,* before the obedient matter and forces and the life-endowment could co-operate to result in the realization of the forms and the population of the globe.

The reason why it is the *essential* part, is, that when once the Divine command issued, the result followed inevitably - that will "go without saying."

In human affairs, also, we speak of the architect having *created* the palace or cathedral, or the ironclad; meaning thereby not the slow process of cutting and joining stone, or riveting steel plates, but the higher antecedent act of mind in evoking the ideal form and providing for all contingencies in the adaptation and subsequent working of the finished structure. And if we limit this use of the term "creation" somewhat in speaking of human works, it is because the concept of the human mind so often fails of realization; that it is one thing to design, and another to accomplish. The grandest design for a palace may fail to stand because some peculiarity of the stone has been forgotten, or some character of foundation and subsoil has been misunderstood. The noblest form of turret-ship may prove useless because the strength of some material will not correspond to the ideal, or some curve of stability has been miscalculated. Not only this: man may create, as a sculptor, the ideal form for his to-be statue, or the dramatist his character; but the perfect realization, either in marble or in an actual being, may be impossible; the ideal remains "in the air." The ideal, therefore, is not the major part of "creation" in a human work.

But with the Divine work it is otherwise. The Divine thought in Creation and its result are separated by no possibility of failure. Given the matter and the laws of force and of life, directly the Great Designer has uttered His thought to those that are His builders, they *must* infallibly and without discord, work through the longest terms, it may be, of an evolutionary series, till, every transitional condition passed, the final form emerges perfect.

Our very verbal definition, admitting as it does "derivative" creation, implies this. We all speak of ourselves as "created." How so? We are not produced ready made. Nor do we wholly solve the matter by saying that we are "created" because we are born from parents who (if we go far enough back) originated in a first production from the hand of Nature. We are really "created" because the *design* - the *life-form of us*, which matter and force were to work together to produce - was the direct product of the Divine Mind.[1]

My question, therefore, of the Genesis interpreters is: Why will you insist on the text meaning only the second element in Creation - the production on earth, and not the Design or its issue in heaven?

The former we could find out some day for ourselves; we *have* found out some of it (though only some) already; the latter we could never know unless we were told. Surely it is the "*dignus vindice nodus*" in this case. To tell us the earth's history within a brief space would be impossible, and would have been for ages unintelligible if it could have been told; to tell us of God's creation is possible - for it has been done; and the record, unless misread, is intelligible for all time.

The narrative, if it is a revelation of Divine Creation in heaven, takes up ground that none can trespass on. None can say "it is not so," unless either he will show that the words will not bear the meaning, or that the context and other Scripture contradict it.

"How did this all first come to be you?
God thought about me and I grew." - *Macdonald.*]

So soon as the matter of earth and heaven (and all that is implied therewith) originated "in the beginning," the narrative introduces to our reverent contemplation the solemn conclave in heaven, when, in a serial order and on separate days, God declared, for the guidance of the ever potentially active forces, and for materials ever (as we know) seeking combination and resolution,[1] the *form* which the earth surface is (it may be ever so gradually) to take and the *life-forms* which are to be evolved.

That this creative work was piecemeal, and on separate days, we know from the narrative. *Why* it was so arranged we do not know. Vast as was the work to be done, almost infinite as was the complexity of the laws required to be formulated, it *could* have all been done at once, in a moment of time; for time does not exist to the Divine Mind. But seeing that the work was to be on earth, and for the benefit of creatures to whom the divisions of time were all-important, we can dimly, at least, discern a certain fitness and appropriateness in the gradual and divided work.

CHAPTER XIV.

THE INTERPRETATION SUPPORTED BY OTHER SCRIPTURES.

In interpreting the narrative before us, we have an important aid which has hardly received the attention it deserves. I allude to the other passages of Scripture which were written by men undoubtedly familiar with the Book of Genesis.

Now, in more than one of them, I find the idea that the Creation spoken of is the *Divine work in heaven*, and not the subsequent and long process of its realization on the surface of our globe, fully confirmed.

In the beautiful thirty-eighth chapter of the very ancient Book of Job, we find a distinct allusion to a time when God "laid the foundations" of the earth, prescribed "its measures," made a "decreed place" for the sea, and framed the "ordinances of heaven," and this in presence of the heavenly host assembled -

"When the morning stars sang together, And all the sons of God shouted for joy.[1]"

The same idea can be gathered from the text which I have placed on the title-page of this book. "By faith we understand that the aeons (the whole system of nature in its various branches, physical, moral, and social) were ordained ([Greek: kataertisthai]) by the word of God." The *process* of actual development is here passed over, as not being the main thing; what attracts attention is the Divine Design, the "framing" of the wonderful ideal or ordinance without which the "aeons" could not proceed to unfold themselves. I do not mean, of course, for a moment to imply that, after God had formulated the laws and designed the forms, He left the working out of the results to themselves. I should be sorry if, in bringing into prominence what has generally been overlooked, I seemed to throw the rest in the shade. God's providence and continued supervision are as important in themselves as the original design: - but this is not the central idea embodied in the passage.

There is another Scriptural allusion which suggests the idea of a Heavenly Conclave, and great act of Creation in heaven. It may be considered somewhat remote, and even fanciful - but the fact is recorded *both* in the Old Testament and the New, and *something* must be meant by it. And, moreover, other and very meaningless interpretations have been from the earliest times given, so that I can hardly omit the subject if I would. I refer to the permanent presence in heaven, around the Divine Throne, of the singular forms of being called *Cherubim*, which seem to indicate some mysterious connection between the life-forms of earth and the inhabitants of heaven, and some permanent representation of typical created forms in heaven. In Ezekiel, chapter i., and again in chapter x., this vision is presented to us.

The prophet was to be prepared, by a very vivid exhibition of the power and glory of God as the Author and Ruler of the universe, to appreciate the depth of degradation to which the Jews had fallen in their rejection of such a God as their Lord and King and of the justice of the terrible overthrow which was the consequence of that rejection.

The vision then displayed (as I understand it) GOD surrounded by the typical forms of creation and the irresistible forces of nature. All forms of life, all energies of nature, were thus shown to be His creatures. There, around the throne, were four "cherubim" of remarkable appearance. They were accompanied by the appearances of fiery orbs like beryl stones, revolving in all directions with ceaseless energy. Any account of this vision that I can give is, however, pitiable beside the inexpressibly sublime picture drawn in Ezekiel, to which I must refer the reader for his own study. And imagine what the feelings of the prophet must have been when, fresh from the impression of this grandeur of Creation - this glory and irresistible power of God as the Centre and great Mover of all, he was taken to witness the pitiable sight of the Jews turning away from His worship, and to see their elders burning incense before walls covered with "every form of creeping things and abominable beasts - all the idols of the house of Israel![1]" How must the vision have prepared him to realize the depth of degradation with which he had to contend, and have fired him with energy to denounce it!

There is, then, I think, considerable probability in the contention that the vision represents God in Creation, surrounded by the types of creation and the forces of nature.

There is, no doubt, the ancient tradition that the four Cherubim meant the four Gospels; and this has now become deeply associated with ecclesiastical symbolism. But I submit that this is only a fancy which can best be left to church embroidery and stained windows; it is unworthy of any serious notice. The beings are described, it will be observed, with great minuteness: all have the same characteristic powers of rapid motion, and all have *human hands*, a fact that so strikes the prophet that he repeats it three times.[2] These four Cherubim, then, seem to me clearly to indicate the archetypes of Creation, the great design-forms of created life, showing themselves the progressive scale from the Animal to the Man and the Angel. And these four great types exactly answer to the resulting groups of created life. We have the development of *Reptilia* into *Birds* as one final type; consequently one face of each cherub has the Bird type - the Eagle head[3]. Two other faces on each give us the *Animal* type, one representing again the great order Carnivora (the Lion), the other the Herbivorous Ungulates (the Ox or Calf); while the fourth face indicates the last development, *Man*.

I would say here, as regards the animal creation being represented by a double form, that it is most curious to notice that this double division of animals is found throughout Scripture, and seems to have its counterpart in the actual facts of creation on earth.

Accompanying these created beings in this remarkable vision were "wheels" which appeared to be spheres within spheres, revolving with ceaseless activity and never turning, but always going forward. The wheels were full of eyes. It appears to me probable that these symbolize - and if so the symbol is at once full of meaning and grandeur - the inevitable, ever wakeful energies and forces of nature, the marvellous agency of electricity, chemical affinity, heat, attraction, repulsion, and so forth. We are accustomed to speak of "blind force;" but here observe the wheels are *full of eyes*, ever vigilant to fulfil the purpose for which they are appointed. And this representation of *forces* appears necessary to complete a symbolic representation of God in nature: since the world is made up of dead matter, of living forms, and of forces or energies which are in ceaseless motion and action, producing the changes which in fact constitute the working of the whole system.

I cannot help thinking, therefore, that the imagery of this vision lend support to the belief that there was a great Creation enacted in heaven, which was followed by the actual carrying out of the processes on earth, *but which has retained its representative forms in the heaven itself.* Had this vision stood alone, it might have been passed over, on the ground that it deals with high and transcendental matters, and that it would be hardly safe to let a practical argument rest too much on it. But the fact is that again in the New Testament a very similar vision is mentioned (in the fourth chapter of the Book of Revelation): here again the four living creatures represent the typical forms of life, the bird, the carnivorous and herbivorous animals, and man; and it will be observed that in this case there is hardly room to doubt that we have an exhibition of *Creation*, for there is express allusion to it in the address of the elders - "Thou hast *created all things*, and for Thy pleasure they are and were created."

CHAPTER XV.

AND SUPPORTED BY THE CONTEXT.

But a step further is necessary: if the conclusion that I have come to, by accepting "day" in its ordinary and natural sense, and by giving a hitherto overlooked (and so far a new) meaning to "creation," is sound, it must not only be rendered probable by reference to other parts of Scripture written when Genesis was much nearer its original publication than it is now; it is still (before all things) necessary, that the interpretation adopted should be conformable to the context.

And I have heard it objected that there are verses which imply not only a Divine Act in heaven, with the Sons of God in conclave around the throne - sublime and wonderful picture! - but also distinctly indicate a corresponding action on earth, and so require us to include in our rendering of "creation" *both* the ideas which (page 169 ante) I have admitted may, on occasion be required by the terms. For example: after the creative command in verses 7, 9, 11, 15, and 24, is declared, it is followed by the words of fulfilment - "and it was so;" and in verse 11, when God has said "Let the earth bring forth grass, &c.", in the next verse it is positively recorded that the earth *did* bring forth grass, &c.

I of course admit all this, but it is in no way opposed to my suggestion.

The *commencement* of the *result* probably, if not necessarily, followed immediately on the issue of the finished command, viz., the promulgation of the forms to be obtained and the processes to be followed. The *whole* result did not become accomplished then and there, in the time mentioned, or exactly in the order mentioned: we know that for a fact. Take, for example, the case of *vegetation*. Here the author, in terms at once precise and universally intelligible, speaks of "vegetation[1]" (grass of the A.V.), "herb yielding seed," and "trees yielding fruit," thereby exhaustively enumerating the members of the vegetable kingdom.

Now, as a matter of fact, there was no one long (or short) period during which the whole of this command was realized, *before* the next creative act occurred.

At first *algae* and low forms of vegetable life appeared; and doubtless we have lost myriads upon myriads of such lower forms of plant-life in the early strata, because such forms were ill calculated for fossil-preservation, owing to the absence of woody fibre, silicious casing, or hard fruit or seed vessels. But when we first have a marked accumulation of specialized plant-life in the coal measures (Upper Carboniferous), it is still only of cryptogams - ferns and great club mosses. A beginning of true seed-bearing plants (Gymnosperm exogens) had been made with the *conifers* of the Devonian strata; but true *grasses*, and the other orders of phanerogamic plants and arboreous vegetation, do not appear till the tertiary rocks were deposited, very long after the age of fish and great reptiles had culminated, and the inauguration of the bird age and the mammalian age had taken place.

Looking only to the abundant, prominent, and characteristic life-forms of the several strata, it could certainly be said that the period when the *water* actually brought forth a vast mass of its life-forms - corals, sertularias, crustaceans, and fish of the lower orders - must have *preceded* (not followed) the time when the earth produced vegetation of all kinds, and further that it must have come after the appearance of scorpions and some land insects.[1]

Moreover, as the regular succession in periods of light and darkness on the earth, and the sequence of seasons was not organized (but only a generally diffused light, and, probably, an uniform and moist state of climate without seasons) till *after* the commands for the formation of the whole of the large classes of plants, both cryptogams and phanerogams, it is obvious that as many of these would require the fuller development of seasonal influences, the whole process could not have been worked out before the fourth day's creative work was begun.

This instance alone - and it would be easy to add others - shows that the narrative cannot be meant to indicate what actually happened on earth, i.e., to summarize the *entire realization* of the Divine command.

Such being the plain facts with regard to the *kind of accomplishment* meant by the terms "it was so," "the earth brought forth," &c., it is quite plain that no violence is done to the text by explaining it as intended to describe what God did in heaven, with the addition, that as each command was formulated, the result on earth surely followed, the thing "was so," and the earth and water respectively no doubt *began* to "bring forth." More than this cannot be made out on *any* interpretation that accords with facts. It seems so clear to me that this is so, that I hardly need refer to the use of the terms the "*waters brought forth*" and the "*earth brought forth*" and the phrase in chapter ii. 5 - the Lord made every plant *before it grew.*

If, as we have been long allowed to suppose, God spake and the water and earth were *at once* fully and finally peopled with animals where before nothing but plants had existed, and so on, I should hardly have expected the use of words which imply a gradual process - a gestation and subsequent birth (so to speak) of life-forms.

How the *order* in which the events are recorded stands in relation to the subsequent history of life-development on earth, and what its significance may be, I will consider later on. First I will conclude the argument for the general interpretation of the narrative.

2. *The Second Genesis Narrative.*

I have only one more direct argument to offer; but I think it is a very important one. The first division of Genesis ends with the Divine commands creating man and the day of rest which followed. The narrative ending at chapter ii. verse 3 (the division of chapters here, as elsewhere, is purely arbitrary), we have at verse 4 of chapter ii, what has been loudly proclaimed as *another* account of *the same* Creation, which, it is added (arbitrarily enough - but *any* argument will do if only it is against religion!) is contrary to the first.[1]

Now, even if there is a *second* account of Creation, it would surely be a circumstance somewhat difficult to explain. *Contrary* in any possible sense, the narrative (from chapter ii. 4, onward) certainly is not. But why should there be a second narrative at all? On the hitherto received supposition that chapter i. intends to tells us the *process* of creation - what God caused to be done on earth, not merely what He did in heaven - there is apparently no room for a second narrative. Nor have I seen any completely satisfactory explanation. But if we accept the view that the first chapter explains the Divine Design, and its being published (so to speak) and commanded in heaven, then it would be very natural that that narrative should be followed by a second, which should detail not the *whole* process of all life existence on earth, but (as the Bible is to be henceforth concerned with Man, his fall and his redemption) with an account of *just so much of the* process as relates to the actual birth on the earth's surface of the particular man Adam, the most important (and possibly not the only) outcome of the *fiat* recorded in chapter i. vers. 27, 28.

In this view, not only *a* second narrative, but just the particular kind of narrative we actually have, is not only natural, but even necessary. *Before*, we had a general account of how God ordained the scheme of material-form and life-form on the earth; *now* we have a detailed account of how He actually carried out one portion of it - that one portion we are most concerned to hear about, namely the man Adam, the progenitor of our own race, of whom came JESUS CHRIST, "the son of Adam.[1]"

The account is designed to introduce to us the scene of Adam's birthplace - the Garden of Eden.[2] The mention of a garden, and the subsequent important connection of the trees of that garden with the conduct of the man, naturally turn the writer's attention to the general subject of the vegetation on the earth's surface. He prefaces his new account accordingly with a brief summary - which I may paraphrase thus without, I trust, departing from the sense of the original: "Such was the origin of the earth (and all in it) and of the heavenly host, at the time when God made them. He had made every plant *before* it was in the earth - every herb of the field *before* it grew" (mark the language as confirming what I have said - God "created" everything before it actually developed and grew into being on the earth). "Rain did not then fall (in the same way as now) on the earth, but the mist that exhaled from the soil re-condensed, and fell and moistened the ground; but there was as yet no MAN to till and cultivate the soil."

Then God actually formed or fashioned *a man*. It is not now that He created the ideal form to be produced in due time, but that He actually formed the individual Adam, and placed him in a garden which He had prepared for the purpose. All the words used now imply actual production. The Divine ideal was ready, and the earth-elements (of which we know man's body to consist) were ready at the Divine word to assume the human shape. And that done, God "breathed into his nostrils the breath of life" (mark the direct *act* on the man himself), and the man became a "living soul." There is nothing here of the "earth bringing forth" as in the former narrative. We have the direct act of God, not in the design only, but in the production of the thing itself.

If this is not a complete explanation and justification of

the second narrative, I do not know what, in common fairness, is entitled to be so called.

The language may be rigorously examined, and it will fully bear out the position taken up.

I conceive, then, that the cumulation of proof need go no further. The true explanation of Genesis i. also supplies the place for Genesis ii. 4, *et seq.*, and overcomes all the difficulty that has hitherto existed on the subject.

It will now, I trust, be clear that by such an interpretation of Genesis we at once give (1) a full and natural meaning to all the terms; we reconcile it with other Scripture, and we enhance all the sublime attributes which we have been reverentially accustomed to connect with this ancient passage. (2) We obviate the difficulty regarding the second narrative in chapter ii. 4. And (3) we place the whole above any possible conflict with science, and above any need for "reconciliation." Here, too, is a purpose and meaning assigned to the *whole* narrative, without being driven into the difficult position of supposing the verses to be the literary outcome of an ignorant imagination which gave expression to its crude ideas only - though enshrining among utterly false details a sublime truth, regarding which one can only wonder why it could not have been stated without the encumbrance of the surroundings.

The naturalist and the biologist may continue, unquestioned, to work out more and more of the wondrous story of Life on the globe. They can never disprove, or on any of their own grounds deny, that God is the Author of all things - matter, force, and mind alike; that He designed the form and relations of the earth; that He organized its light, its seasons, and its changes; that He has furnished the types and patterns of all life-forms which matter and force are conformably thereto, developing on the earth. In short, REVELATION tells us that God did all this "in the beginning," how His form-designs were thought out and declared in six days, and how He rested on the seventh day.

SCIENCE will tell us how, when, and where the Creative fiats and the designs of heaven were realized and worked out on earth.

Here is the separate province of each, without fear of clashing, or room for controversy.

CHAPTER XVI.

THE DETAILS OF THE CREATION NARRATIVE.

Sec.1. *The Explanation of the Verses.*

It remains only now to go over the narrative, the *general* bearing of which I have thus endeavoured to vindicate, so that minor matters of detail, in which it is supposed (1) that some contradiction to known physical fact may still lurk, and (2) something that negatives the explanation suggested, may be cleared up.

Let us take it seriatim: -

"In the beginning God created the heaven (plural in the original) and the earth."

As I have before remarked, we have no real need to discuss whether "bara" means originated (created where nothing previously existed), or whether we should render it "fashioned," i.e., moulded material (thus assumed in terms to be) already in existence.

Either will yield perfectly good and consistent sense; but, as a matter of fact, there is a virtual consensus of the best scholars that the word is here used to denote original production of the material.

It is also clear that the text is intended to embrace the whole system of planets, suns, stars, and whatever else is in space. So the Psalmist understood it: "By the word of the Lord were the heavens made, and *all* the host of them by the breath of his mouth.[1]" Nor is there any reasonable doubt, exegetically, that the subsequent allusion to the sun, moon, and stars, refers (as the sense of the text itself obviously requires) to their *appointment* or adjustment to certain relations with the earth, and assumes their original material production in space, to have been already stated or understood.

"And the earth was (became) without form[2] and void, and darkness was upon the face of the deep. And the Spirit of God moved upon the face of the waters."

I have, in another connection, already remarked on this verse, and so shall not repeat those remarks.

I will only say that the elemental strife and rushing together of chemical elements under the stress of various forces and the presence of enormous heat, would naturally envelop the globe in dense vapours, a large portion of which would be watery vapour, capable of condensation or of dispersion, under proper conditions, afterwards to be prescribed and realized. As it is beautifully expressed in Job xxxviii., "When I made the cloud the garment thereof, and thick darkness a swaddling-band for it" (verse 8).

Then commences the serial order of Divine acts with reference to the *Earth*: -

(1) "AND GOD SAID; LET THERE BE LIGHT: AND THERE WAS LIGHT."

This verse is commonly taken as indicating a creation of light for the first time in the entire cosmos or universe. And if it be so, there is no objection, on any scientific ground, to the assertion that there was once a time when as yet the vibrations and waves which we connect with the idea of Light, had not yet begun. It is true that nebular matter, as now observed, is believed to be, partially at any rate, self-luminous. But this fact, supposing it to be such, is not inconsistent with a still earlier time when light had not yet begun. From the "wave-theory" of light, which is one of those working hypotheses which are indispensable, and which, in a sense, may be said to be demonstrated by their indispensability, it can clearly be seen that if light is caused by rapid vibrational movement, there must have been - or at any rate there is nothing against an authoritative declaration that there was - a moment of time when the first vibrational impulse was given, when, in fact, God said "Let there be light, and there was light," *before* which also there was "darkness upon the face of the deep.[1]"

There is no necessary connection between the creation of light *per se*, and the existence of any particular source (or sources) of light to our planet or to other planets.

No justification is now needed for such a remark, and the almost forgotten cavils of one of the "Essays and Reviews" may still survive as a "scientific" curiosity, to warn us against too hastily concluding that (in subjects where so little is really *known*) the Bible must be wrong, and the favourite hypothesis of the day right.

But as a matter of fact, the text, especially when read in connection with Job xxxviii., need not be taken to refer to any original creation of light in the universe generally, but merely to the letting in of light on the hitherto dark and "waste" earth. The command "Let there be light" was followed on the next day by the formation of a firmament or expanse. So that all the verse *necessarily* implies is, that the thick clouds and vapours which surrounded the earth were so dealt with, that light could reach the earth: the light was thus divided from the darkness, and the rotating globe would experience the alternation of day and night.

The "day" having thus been created formally (so to speak), the Divine Author proceeds to mark, by His own Procedure, the use of the "days" which He had provided for the earth.

On this view, of course, the origin of light as a "force" - the first beginning of its pulsations - is not detailed, any more than the origin of electric force, or heat, or gravitation.

Here, too, I may remark that the idea of *creation*, which it has been one of my chief objects to develop, is illustrated. This remark holds good, whether an original creation of light is intended, or only an arrangement whereby light was for the first time introduced to the earth's surface. The idea of creating light not only involves the Divine Conception of the thing, and the marvellous method of its production,[1] but doubtless, also, all those wonderful laws of reflection, refraction, polarization, and a thousand others, which the science of Physical Optics investigates.

Naturally enough, in this case, the double idea involved in creation - the Divine concept and its realization - will, in the nature of things, fall into one. No process of evolution is required; none is indicated by science. Directly the Divine hand gave the impulse concurrently with the Divine thought - light would be. In the nature of things there is no place for a line between the Divine fiat and its realization, as there is in the production of life-forms on the earth. Or, on the other view, directly the Divine command went forth, the vapours would clear and allow the transmission of light.

(2) "AND GOD SAID, LET THERE BE A FIRMAMENT (EXPANSE) IN THE MIDST OF THE WATERS, AND LET IT DIVIDE THE WATERS FROM THE WATERS....AND GOD CALLED THE FIRMAMENT HEAVEN."

There has been gathered round this verse what I may call rather an ill-natured controversy, because there is no real ground for it; and the objections taken seem rather of a desire to find out something against the narrative at any price, than to make the best of it. The verse, when duly translated, implies that an "expanse" - the setting of a clear space of atmosphere around the globe - formed one of the special design-thoughts of the Creator, followed by its immediate (or gradual) accomplishment. I think we should have hardly had so much cavilling over this word "expanse" if it had not been for the term subsequently used by the Seventy in their Greek version ([Greek: stereoma]). The ancients, it is said, believed the space above the earth to be "solid."

Now I would contend that even if the Hebrew writer had any mistaken or confused notions in his own mind, that would not afford any just ground against revelation itself. But I would point out that many of the expressions which may be quoted to show the idea of solidity, are clearly poetical. And if we go to the poetic or semi-poetic aspect of things, may I not ask whether there is not a certain sense in which the earth-envelope may be said to be solid? The air has a considerable density, its uniform and inexorable pressure on every square inch of the earth's surface is very great. Such a word as [Greek: stereoma] (*firmamentum*) does not imply solidity in the sense in which gold is solid - as if the heavens were a mass of metal, and the stars set in it like jewels; it implies, rather, something fixed and offering resistance.

It is obvious that a creative act was necessary for this "expanse." We know of spheres that have no atmosphere; and we are so ignorant of the true nature of what is beyond the utmost reach of our air-stratum, that there is room for almost any consistent conjecture regarding it.

Moreover, observe that the atmosphere is not a *chemical* combination of gases, and one, therefore, that would take place like any other of the metallic, saline, or gaseous combinations, of which no detailed account is given - all being covered by the general phrase, "God created the heaven and the earth." The air is a mechanical mixture, pointing to a special design and a special act of origin. The necessary proportions of each gas and its combined properties could not have originated without guidance.

But the main purpose of the expanse, as stated in the text, was to regulate the water supply. That vast masses of watery vapour must at one time have enveloped the globe, seems probable - apart from revelation; and that part of this should condense into seas and fresh-water, and part remain suspended to produce all the phenomena of invisible air-moisture and visible cloud, while an "expanse" was set, so that the earth surface should be free, and that light might freely penetrate, and sound also, and that all the other regular functions of nature dependent on the existing relation of earth and air should proceed - all this was very necessary. And when we recollect what a balanced and complex scheme it is - how very far from being a simple thing; we recognize in the adjustment of earth's atmospheric envelope, a special result worthy of the day's work.

Whether the separation between the condensed but ever re-evaporating and re-condensing water on the earth's surface, and the water vapour in the atmosphere, is *all* that is meant by the division of the "waters that are above the firmament" from those below, it would not be wise to assert. We know so little of the condition of space beyond our own air, and so little of the great stores of hydrogen which have been suggested to exist in space (and might combine to form vast quantities of liquid), that we may well leave the phrase as it stands, content with a partial explanation.

(3) "AND GOD SAID, LET THE WATERS UNDER THE HEAVEN BE GATHERED TOGETHER UNTO ONE PLACE, AND LET THE DRY LAND APPEAR: AND IT WAS SO. AND GOD SAID, LET THE EARTH PUT FORTH GRASS (VEGETATION), HERB YIELDING SEED, AND FRUIT TREE BEARING FRUIT AFTER ITS KIND, WHEREIN IS THE SEED THEREOF."

The only remarks that the first part of this verse calls for, are, first, that it explains how far from mere chance-work the emergence of land from the water was; *second* how well it illustrates the use of terms relating to creation.

The whole scheme of the distribution of the surface of earth into land and water is one which demanded Divine foresight and a complete ideal[1] which was to be attained by the action and reaction of natural forces, just as much as the production of the most specialized form of plant-or animal-life.

This is not the place to go into detail as to how much of the world's life-history and its climatic conditions depend on the distribution of land and water. It is sufficient to recognize the immense importance of that distribution.

But, in the second place, it will be observed that while it is natural to suppose (though not logically necessary) that the working out of the Divine plan *commenced* immediately on the issue of the Divine command and the declared formulation of the Divine scheme, yet we know - few things are better known - that the whole scheme was not completely realized in one day, or one age - certainly not *before* there was any appearance of plant-life, aquatic, or dry land, or any appearance of animal-life.

I believe (though I have lost my reference) it is held by some authorities that the position of the great *oceans* as they are now (and omitting, of course, all minor coast variations) has been fixed from very early geologic times. But, apart from that, we have ample evidence of whole continents arising and being again submerged; and of continual changes between land and water of the most wide-reaching character again and again happening during the progress of the world's history. So that here we may see clearly an instance where the revelation of the creative act must be held to refer to the great primal design - teaching us that it is a fact that at first all *was* laid down, foreseen, and designed by the Creator; but not referring to anything like an account of the *results* upon earth, which, for aught we know to the contrary, may not yet be complete.

As to the second part of the text, we are here introduced to the commencement of life-forms on earth.

No separation is recorded. Directly the chemical elements of matter have so combined that a solid earth and liquid water (salt and fresh) are formed, and the cooling process has gone on sufficiently long to enable the dense vapours partly to settle down and condense, partly to remain as vapour (dividing the waters above from the waters below) - directly this process is aided by the admission of diffused light and by the adjustment of the atmosphere, and the superficial adjustment of the distribution of water and land surface is provided for, then plant-life is organized.

It will be observed that even aquatic plants and algae though growing in or under water, are nevertheless connected with the *earth*; so that the phrase, "Let the *earth* bring forth," is by no means inappropriate.

The earliest rock deposits are able to tell us little about the first beginning of plant-life. Moreover, as animal-life began only with the interval of one day (the fourth), we should expect to find - on the supposition that the heavenly *fiat* at once received the *commencement* of its fulfilment on each day - that the first lowly specimens of vegetable and animal life are almost coeval. And this is (apparently) the fact.

It is to be remarked that plant and animal always appear in nature as two separate and *parallel* kingdoms. It is not that the plant is lower than the animal, so that the highest plant takes on it some of the first characters which mark the lowest animal: but both start separately from minute and little specialized forms so similar that it is extremely difficult to say which is plant and which is animal.[1]

All the beginnings of life in *either* kingdom would therefore be ill-adapted (most of them, at any rate) for preservation in rock-strata.[1]

All we know for certain is that vegetable-life was closely coeval with the lowest animal-life, and that it was very long before specialized forms, even of *cryptogams*, made a great show in the world.

Probability is entirely in favour of the actual priority being in vegetable forms; and more than that is not required. For the Mosaic narrative, while it places the origin of the vegetable kingdom actually first, lets the *fiat* for the animal kingdom follow almost immediately.

As to the *order* of appearance of the plants, I will reserve my remarks for the moment.

(4) "AND GOD SAID, LET THERE BE LIGHTS IN THE FIRMAMENT OF THE HEAVEN, TO DIVIDE THE DAY FROM THE NIGHT; AND LET THEM BE FOR SIGNS, AND FOR SEASONS, AND FOR DAYS, AND FOR YEARS: AND LET THEM BE

FOR LIGHTS IN THE FIRMAMENT TO GIVE LIGHT ON THE EARTH."

The sun and the stars, and all the host of heaven, are clearly understood to have been created "in the beginning," under the general statement of fact which forms the first verse of the narrative.

The 14th verse has always been understood to refer to the establishment of the *relations* between the earth and the sun, moon, and stars, which have, as a matter of fact, been recognized by all ages and all people ever since. The writer of the 104th Psalm certainly so understood the passage -

> "He appointed the moon for seasons;
> The sun knoweth his going down.[1]"

The writer was instructed to use popularly intelligible language, and so the text speaks of the lights as they *appear* in the sky or firmament.

Even if we suppose that before this act, the sun was already incandescent, and the moon capable of reflecting the light, the whole arrangement of the earth's rotation may have been such that the alternations of light and darkness may have been very different from what they are now, and the seasons also. A moment's reflection regarding the obliquity of the earth's axis, nutation, the precession of the equinoxes, the eccentricity of the orbit and the changes in the position of the orbit, will show us what ample room there was for a special adjustment and adaptation between the earth and its satellite and between both to the solar centre.[2] So that faith which accepts this as a Divine arrangement made among the special and formal acts of Creation, cannot be said to be unreasonable, or to be flying in the face of any known facts.

It is very remarkable, as showing how little we can attribute this narrative, on any basis of probability, to mere fancy or guess-work, that this matter should have been assigned to the fourth day - *after* the fiat for plant-life had gone forth.

But the fact is that the unregulated light, and the vaporous uniform climate that must have continued if the fourth day's command had never issued, though it might have served for a time for the lowest beginnings of life, especially marine or aquatic, would ultimately have rendered any advance in the series of design impossible. Such a fact would never have occurred to an ignorant and uninspired writer.

It is here impossible to say whether the whole arrangements indicated were made at once in obedience to the Divine Design, or were produced gradually.

It has been suggested that uniformity of climate and temperature continued up till the carboniferous ages, at any rate; and it is only in the later ages that such differences of *fauna* in different parts of the world appear, as to show differences of climate more like what we have at present.

Whether this is so or not, I am not concerned to argue. The narrative tells us that God did, at a certain point in his Creative work, design and ordain the necessary arrangements; and physical science may find out, when it is able, how and when the adjustments spoken of came about.

(5) AND GOD SAID -
> (i.) Let the waters bring forth the moving creature that hath life,
> (ii.) Let fowl fly above the earth on the face of the expanse.

As to (i.) the "creation" consisted of - great sea-monsters (or water monsters), and every living thing that moveth.

Then the animal life received a *blessing*. Animals, even the lowliest, are capable of a new feature in life - happiness in their being, which cannot be predicated of plants.

(6) AND GOD SAID -
> (i.) Let the earth bring forth the living creature after its kind ... the beast of the earth *after its kind (Carnivora)*, cattle *after its kind (Ungulata)*, and everything that creepeth on the ground *after its kind*.[1]

And also -

> (ii.) Let us make man.... So God created man in His own image - in the image of God created He him; male and female created He them.

(7) Then followed the day of rest.

Sec. 2. *The Order of Events considered.*

It was convenient first to bring these later Creative Acts together before beginning any remarks about any one of them.

It will now be desirable to notice what occurred, because here the question of *order* is concerned. I could not avoid a partial statement on this subject at an earlier page, nor would it be quite sufficient simply to refer the reader back to those pages. At the risk of some repetition, I will therefore consider the subject here. It will be observed that on the older interpretation, which passed over the special act of God in *designing* and *publishing the design,* and descended at once to the earth to the process of producing the designed forms, this order was matter of great importance.

Granting the supporters of this view that the six days are unequal periods often of vast duration, with or without important subdivisions, they are bound to make out that each creation began, and was at any rate well advanced, *before* the next began. We ought, in fact, to see a period more or less prolonged when the whole of what is indicated in the *plant* verse was well advanced, *before* any marine or fresh-water life appeared at all.[1]

All attempts to make out that this *was* so, have proved failures. It is assumed, for instance (and justly so), that life on the globe began with low vegetable forms; these represented the "grass" of the text, and it is suggested that the "fruit tree" is represented by the Devonian and Carboniferous *conifers*. This in itself is a very strained view. It is recollected that the terms used are not scientific, but for the world at large; but without confining "fruit tree" to mean only trees having *edible* fruit, still the appearance of a few first species of *conifers* in the Devonian, can hardly be called an adequate fulfilment of the requirements of the passage. But even so, myriads of fish and other animals existed *before* the Devonian and Carboniferous plant age.

The animal forms that so existed, have therefore to be *ignored*, or are assumed to have been created without special notice: and it is said that the Mosaic period of "moving creatures of the deep," fishes and monsters, only began when the rocks begin to show *great abundance* of shells, of fish, and subsequently of huge reptilians which prepared the way for birds - which gradually make their appearance towards the Trias.

But the Devonian "age of fishes" (Devonian including old red sandstone) was far too important a period to be thus got rid of; and it is difficult to understand *why* the narrative should exclude all the extensive and beautiful (though often little specialized) orders of marine life - all the Corals, the Mollusca and Articulata, which had long abounded - especially some of the Crustaceans, not an unimportant group of which (*Trilobite*[1]) had also culminated and almost passed away before the Devonian; to say nothing of the fact that *land* "creeping things" (scorpions among *crustacea*, and apparently winged insects) had occurred.

It is a special difficulty also, that if *insects* are included among the "creeping things" of the *earth* then various families of the "land-creation" (sixth day) became represented *before* the great reptiles of the "water-creation" (fifth day).

The fact is that a glance at the subjoined Tables (which are only generally and approximately correct) will suffice to show how the main features of the progress of life-forms differ from what is required by the older methods of reading Genesis. To reduce the table within limits, I have grouped together all the lower forms of life in the animal table, viz., the sponges, corals, encrinites, and molluscs. It is sufficient to say that these appear in all the rocks except the very oldest - the Caelenterata beginning, and the Molluscoids exhibiting an early order in *brachiopoda*, which seems to be dying out. Crustaceans and insects appeared as early as Silurian times.

The idea of successive "kingdoms" or "periods," each of which was *complete* in its actual fauna upon earth before the next was fully ushered in, can no longer be defended.

It is in the *completion* of one class of life before the other, that the fallacy of the period theory lies - for completion is essential to that theory which supposes "the Mosaic author" to have intended to describe the *process of production on earth.*

But it is quite impossible to deny that there *is* a certain observable movement and gradual procession in the history of life which is exactly consistent with what is most likely to have happened, supposing the Divine designs of life-forms were first declared in successive order at short intervals of time, and then that the processes of nature worked out the designs in the fulness of time and gradually in order, each one *beginning* before the next, but only beginning.

I do not deny that it is perfectly *conceivable* that the Creator might have designed the forms in one order, and that the actual production or evolution of the corresponding living creatures might not have been (for reasons not understood) exactly, or even at all, coincident with the order.

But it is impossible to deny the strong feeling of probability that the commands would *begin* to be worked out, in the order in which they were uttered.

And here it is that the correspondence which undoubtedly exists, gives rise to controversy.

From one point of view it is just enough to encourage the "period" holders to try and arrange a scheme; but it is just hot enough to prevent their opponents (justly) taxing them with straining or "torturing" the text and failing fairly to make out their case after all. From another point of view the correspondence is so far established, and so undeniably unprecedented (in human cosmogonies) and noteworthy, as to demand imperatively our careful consideration and compel us to account for it.

It will be observed, first of all, that the whole "creation" (omitting all incidental and preparatory works) is stated in *groups* each having an order within itself.

Group 1.   God created (both land and water) "vegetation" - plants yielding seed, fruit-trees.

Group 2.   In water, not necessarily excluding *amphi-bia*: - Great aquatic monsters; fish and all other creatures that move. In air: - Winged fowl.

Group 3.   On land generally - for some forms are amphibious: - Beasts (*Carnivora*), cattle (*Ungulata*, &c.), and other things that creep on the ground (the smaller and lower forms of life collectively).

The order *within* the groups is evidently of no

consequence, because the writer does not adhere to it in two consecutive verses dealing with the same subject; while the "versions" seem to point to some variations in the text itself as to arrangement, though not as to substance.

But as regards the order *of* the groups themselves, it is, as I said, very natural (but yet not logically inevitable) to expect that when the results came to be existent on earth, those results should exhibit a sequence corresponding to the order in which the groups were created. And it is never denied (in *any* of the most recent publications[1]) that to this extent nature confirms the belief.

I am aware that Professor Huxley's recent articles may at first sight seem to go against this; but that is not so on any grounds of actual fact, but of a particular *interpretation* - which I submit is wholly unwarranted.

For instance, it is insisted that the "sea-monsters" of the second group included *sirenia* and *cetacea* (dugongs, manatees, and whales, dolphins, &c.), which are mammals. In that case a portion of the command would not have been obeyed - a number of the designed forms would have been kept in abeyance - for a long time. And the same is still more true if bats - a highly placed group of mammals - were included in "winged fowl."

But both these interpretations are distinctly arbitrary, incapable of holding good, and also entirely ignore the conditions of a Revelation.

The narrative is not discussed or defended as an ordinary secular narrative, which is true according to the *writer's uninspired intention or the state of his personal knowledge*. It is defended as a Revelation. The distinction is as obvious as it is important, directly a moment's consideration is accorded.

If we assume, for a moment, that God *did* (on any theory whatever of Inspiration) instruct, direct, or enable the writer in making the record, then it is obvious that the writer either put down what he saw in a vision, or what was in some other manner borne on his mind. In any case, he could have had no critical knowledge, and no historical knowledge as an eye-witness, of the actual facts; and he may very well therefore have used language the full meaning of which he did not apprehend.[1] What alone is essential is, that the narrative as it stands, on an ordinary critical, linguistic, and grammatical interpretation, should not contain anything which is untrue. Suppose, for example, the word "tanninim" to be *incapable* of bearing any other meaning linguistically than "cetacean," then the narrative might be objected to; but if it will bear a meaning which is consistent with fact, then it is no matter that the writer at the time had an erroneous, or (what is more likely) no defined, idea in his own mind of the meaning. And so with "winged fowl" - the objection fails entirely, unless it can be shown, not only that the writer might have thought "bats" to be included, *but* that linguistically the word *cannot have* any other meaning than one which would include bats.[2]

We have every right, then, to say that the "tanninim" of the text may be taken to refer to that great and remarkable age of Saurians which is not only of very great importance in itself, but becomes doubly so when we see its connection backward with the fishes, and forward through the Pterodactyles to Odontoformae (*Apatornis* and *Icthyornis*) and modern winged birds (*Hesperonis* for the Penguins); and through the Dinosaurs[1] with the Saurornithes, with the *Dinornis* and the struthious birds; and through the Theriodonts with the mammalian *carnivora*.

In that case the sequence of the two groups, plants and aquatic animal-forms, is explained. They come almost together - plants being probably actually the first, and mollusca, fishes, and saurians.

There is, further, no real dispute that the Saurians led up to the Aves, and that the third group (of mammals) follows all the members of the second group. The earliest known mammal (*microlestes*) is an isolated forerunner of not very certain location, the real bulk of the mammalian orders beginning in the Eocene. Seeing, too, how very closely one Creative command is recorded to have followed on the other, it is not in any way against the narrative that some land forms of crustaceans and insects (and possibly others) began to appear at an early stage, when the vegetable and water-animal forms had only progressed as far as the Silurian and Devonian ages. Nor should we wonder if mammalian forms had occurred earlier. I mention this because of the evident gap in the geologic record between the Cretaceous and the Eocene, and because in the article of December, 1885 (and elsewhere), Professor Huxley has used language which suggests that mammals may have existed of which the rocks give no sign. E.g. (p. 855): "The organization of the bat, bird, or pterodactyle, presupposes that of a terrestrial quadruped ... and is intelligible only as an extreme modification of the organization of a terrestrial *mammal or* reptile." The italics are of course mine. And again (p. 855), "I am not aware that any competent judge would hesitate to admit that the organization of these animals (whales, dugongs, &c.) shows the most obvious signs of their descent from terrestrial quadrupeds."

I do not quote these words of so great a master as presuming to question them (even if, as a scientific verdict, I had any motive for so doing), but merely to point out as a matter of plain and fair reasoning, that if a Divine Creator had designed certain forms to be gradually attained by the processes of Evolution, it would not be necessary that any actually realized form or tangible creature should have existed as ancestors. Logically, the necessity is *either* that certain animals should have actually existed whose descendants gradually lost or gained certain features and functions till the forms we are speaking of resulted, *or* that certain patterns or designs should have been created according to which development proceeded by regular laws till the forms in question resulted.

A few words as to the terms used in describing the contents of each group, may be added. It is obvious that the terms are intended to be exhaustive of certain main groups which are described sufficiently, without being cast in a form which would have been incompatible with the use (at the time) of a human agent as the medium of the recorded Revelation.

(1) "Vegetation" (of an indefinite character, but not bearing seed), plants bearing seed, trees bearing fruit with the seed in it - certainly exhaust the entire range of plant-life.

(2) Moving creatures that live (and fish are afterwards

expressly mentioned) and great monsters (tann[i=]n[i=]m), cover the entire field of life up to Reptilia as far as these are aquatic forms.

(3) The terms used for the third group are also obviously exhaustive - the separate mention of the *cattle* and the *beast* (Carnivora and Ungulates) is a form which is invariably noticed throughout the Old and New Testaments. The "creeping things" would include all minor forms, all land reptiles not described above as the "tann[i=]n[i=]m," and insects.

And it is remarkable that the tortoises, the snakes, and, the more modern forms of crocodile and lizard, and the amphibia and higher insects, are all cainozoic - some of them were preceded by more or less transitory representatives, e.g., the Carboniferous *Eosaurus* and Permian *Protosaurus* the ancient Labyrinthodons and Urodelas, Chelonians and the amphicaelian crocodiles. Snakes have no palaeozoic representative.

Land insects, as might naturally be expected, go back to the times when land vegetation was sufficiently established, and appear gradually all along the line from the Silurian onwards. The modern types, however, are Tertiary.

The succession, we observe, may be illustrated by the resemblance of a number of arrows shot rapidly one after the other in so many parallel courses: all would soon be moving nearly together.

Plant-life, the subject of the first Divine designing, has, as far as we can reasonably say, the start. According to known laws it appears in elementary and undeveloped forms, and gradually progresses. One group

(Cryptogams) reaches a magnificent development and begins to die away in point of grandeur, though still abundantly exemplified. Phanerogamic plants in their lowest groups of gymnosperm exogens then begin to appear in the Devonian conifers, gradually followed by *cycads*. And it is not till Cainozoic times that we have the endogenous grasses and palms and angiospermous exogens.

But the command regarding animal life had followed the other after a short interval, so that we soon see this developing *pari passu* with the other groups - first the lower marine forms and gradually advancing to the Pisces, Amphibia, Reptilia, and then to Aves, as a special division in the second great design group. Lastly the mammals appear and man.[1] But throughout all, we see the rise, culmination, and decay of many transitory and apparently preparatory groups - such as, for example, the Labyrinthodons and Urodelas - preceding the modern types of Amphibia; ancient fish-forms preceding modern ones, and either dying out or leaving but a few and distant representatives; or again, the whole tribes of ancient Saurians, of which something has already been said. All these wonderful under-currents and cross-currents, rises and falls, appearances and disappearances, nevertheless all work together till the whole earth is peopled with the forms , designed in the beginning by the Heavenly Creator.

No account of Creation can be other than wonderful and mysterious; nor can the mystery of the Divine act be explained in language other than that of analogy.

We can speak without mystery of a human architect conceiving a design in his mind; and when he utters it, it is by putting the plans and details upon paper, and handing them over to the builders, who set to work (under the architect's supervision, and in obedience to all the rules he has prescribed as to the methods of work and materials to be used).

All this we can transfer by analogy only, to a Divine design. The design is in the Divine mind, and He utters it in no material plans or drawings: the forces of nature and the chemical elements, His obedient builders, have no hands to receive the plans or eyes to scan them; but we can perceive the analogy directly, and that is all that is necessary for Faith.

The origin of all we see in the world and in the entire Cosmos is, then, in God; and as regards the adjustments of our globe and its relations, and the actual life-forms in plant and animal, they came into existence pursuant to groups of types or designs, made by the Divine Mind, and declared by Him from His Throne in heaven, in six several days - periods of the rotation of our earth.

That is the message of Revelation. It requires no straining of the sacred text: it takes everything as it stands, and the seemingly lengthy explanation it requires is not to manipulate the text, but to clear away the heap of mistaken conceptions that have gathered round it: - to establish the idea, that the terms "God said, Let there be," and so forth, mean Heaven work, in the design and type - not earth work in its realization and building up. Establishing this by illustration and argument, nothing more is required in the way of textual exegesis except to argue for the rejection of perverse and unsustainable meanings long given to "days," to " expanse " or " firmament," and to "great whales" in the narrative.

It will be admitted readily that if this account of Creation is the true one, if the meaning assigned to the Genesis narrative is correct, it affords no hindrance to *any* conclusions that may progressively be demanded by the investigation of life-history on earth.

It requires us to believe that the forms which life assumes are not chance forms, nor the *unpremeditated* results of environment and circumstance. But we are not told positively which forms are transitory, which are final.

It is only a matter of probable opinion, which it is quite open to any one to dispute, that there is any indication of finality. I should personally be inclined to think that we have indications that carnivora, ungulates, and birds are final forms; that no evolution will ever modify a bird further into anything that is not a bird; that no transition between the ungulates and the carnivora is possible; that the *proboscideae* are not a final but a transitory type, dying out gradually - our elephants and similar forms will disappear as the mastodon did.

But I admit this is all mere speculation, in which I ask no one to follow me.

On one important point only is there a difference; and if the text is ever proved wrong on that, it must be given up. But it is here that all scientific knowledge fails, in *any way whatever,* to touch the sacred text. There *is* an unique and exceptional account of one "special creation." A man "Adam" is described as having been actually created, not born as an ultimately modified descendant of ancestors originally far removed from himself. That is not to be denied; not only was his bodily form specially created (conformably to the *type* created in Genesis i. 26), but a special spiritual and higher life was imparted - for I believe that no one disputes this as the meaning of the expression, "breathed into his nostrils the *breath of lives,* and man became a living soul."

It must be noted again - although I have before alluded to this in some detail - that it is not impossible that, pursuant to the general command "Let us make man," there *may* have been other human creations, perhaps not endowed with the higher life of Adam. If it is found difficult to realize this because the *image of God* is connected (from the very first) with the design of Man's life-form, still it is to be remembered as an undeniable fact, that the form, though one assumed by God Himself in the Incarnation, *is connected* in structure and function with the general animal (Mammalian) type, and that even the Adamic or spiritually endowed man *may*, by neglecting the higher and giving way to the lower nature, develop much of the purely bestial in himself. So that the bare possibility of a pre-Adamite and imperfect man cannot be *a priori* denied. More than that it is not necessary to say. Nor is it necessary that any origin of man should be limited to six or eight thousand years back. If the state of the text is such that a perfect chronology is possible,[1] then all that the Bible goes back to chronologically is the particular man Adam. And it is quite impossible that any scientific or historical contradiction can arise therefrom.

APPENDIX.

PROFESSOR DELITZSCH ON THE GARDEN OF EDEN.

The information here put together is a compilation from papers in "The Nineteenth Century," and other sources. It has no pretentions to originality, but only to give a brief and connected account of the subject, more condensed and freed from surrounding details than that which the original sources afford.

Before entering on the subject, I would again call attention to the surpassing importance of these early chapters of Genesis. And, I add, that unbelievers are especially glad to be able to allege anything they can against them, because they are aware that hardly any chapters in the Bible are more constantly alluded to, and made the foundation of practical arguments by our Lord and His Apostles, than these early chapters in the Divine volume. If these chapters can be shown to be mythical, then the divine knowledge of our Lord, as the Son of God, and the inspiration of His Apostles, are put in question. All through the Old Testament, allusions to Adam and to the early history in Genesis occur; and among other passages, I will only here invite attention to the 31st chapter of Ezekiel, where there is, in a most beautiful description of the cedar-tree, an allusion to "Eden, the Garden of God" (see also chapter xxviii. ver. 13), which some have thought to indicate that the site was still known, and existing in the time of the prophet. This at least may be remarked, that in verse 9, where the prophet speaks of the "trees that *were* in the Garden of God," the word *were* is not in the original, and the sense of the context would rather denote the present tense - "the trees that *are* in the Garden of God."

But it is in the New Testament that the most repeated and striking allusions to Adam, the temptation of the woman by the Serpent, and the entrance of sin and death into the life-history of mankind, occur.[1]

As regards the narrative of Eden itself, there has been, from the very earliest times, some disposition to regard it as mystical or "allegorical," i.e., to regard it as representing spiritual facts of temptation and disobedience, under the guise or story of an actual audible address by a serpent, and the eating of an actual fruit. The earliest translators seem to have glossed the "Gan-'Eden," everywhere in the Old Testament (*except* in Gen. ii. 8), by the phrase "the paradise of pleasure," or some other similar term. And the Vulgate *always* uses some phrase, such as "place of delight," "voluptas," "deliciae," &c. It must be admitted that there is some temptation to this course, because of the inveterate tendency of the human mind to reduce things to its own level - to suppose everything to have happened *in ways which are within its present powers to comprehend.* We figure to ourselves the fear and dislike *we* should ourselves experience, of a large snake; we imagine the amazement with which an intelligible voice would be heard to proceed from such a creature; so far from being *tempted, we* should at once be moved to hostility or to flight; and thus we are inclined to throw doubt on the narrative as it stands.

But this is to do what we justly complain of modern materialists and positivists for doing - reducing everything to terms of present experience and knowledge.

It has to be borne in mind, that *under the conditions of the case*, the serpent was neither ugly, dangerous,nor loathsome, but beautiful and attractive; that the residents of the Garden were familiar with the "voice of God" - i.e., they had habitual intelligible communication with heaven: probably, also, free intercourse with angelic messengers (inconceivable as it may now seem to us) was matter of daily experience to them. The woman would then recognize in the voice an Angel communication; and unaware at first that it was an evil angel, it would excite no surprise in her at all. Sensations of terror, surprise, dislike, and so forth, were *ex hypothesi* unknown. Why then should not the narrative be exact, unless, indeed, we have some *a priori* ground for supposing that human nature *never could* have been in a state where the voice of God and angels sounded in its ears, and where innocence and the absence of all evil emotion was the daily condition of life? The unbeliever may sneer at such a state, but *reason* why it should *not* have been, he can give none. So, again, with the idea of the "tree of the knowledge of good and evil" and the "tree of life." We are no doubt tempted to think that these terms may be symbolic; but a more careful reflection, and a deliberate rejection of the *influence of present experiences*, may lead us to accept the narrative more literally. Even now, we are not unfamiliar with the ideas of medicinal virtues in plants and fruits. I see nothing impossible in the idea that God may have been pleased to impart such virtue to the fruit of a tree standing in the midst of the Garden, that physical health, immunity from all decay, and constant restoration, should have been the result of eating the fruit; and the eating of this fruit, we know, was freely permitted. The late Archbishop Whately suggested, and I think with great probability, that the longevity of the earliest generations of the Adamic race may have been due to the beneficial effects of the eating of this fruit, which only gradually died out. Just as we know at the present time, that peculiarities introduced into human families, often survive from father to son, till they gradually die out after many generations.

Again, as regards the "forbidden tree," it will not seem impossible, that as a simple *test of obedience* in a very primitive state, the rule of abstinence from a particular fruit may have been literally enjoined, and that the consequence of the moral act of *disobedience* (rather than the physical effect of the fruit eaten) should have been the knowledge of evil, the first sensation of shame, terror, angry dissension, and, worst of all, the alienation from God the source of all good, which followed.

All such considerations of the reality of the history must gain greatly in strength, if we can demonstrate that the Garden of Eden, the scene of the temptation, the place where the trees that were the vehicles of such consequences to the occupants of the garden, stood, had a real existence and geographical site. Now I need hardly remark that the Mosaic narrative unquestionably *professes* a geographical exactness and a literal existence of the garden, as no fabled locality - no Utopia or garden of the Hesperides. I need only refer to the *data* afforded to us by Gen. ii. 8-14.

The Lord, it is said, planted a garden in Eden: it was "eastward;" but that does not directly indicate its site. From Gen. iv. 16, we also learn that the land of Nod where Cain dwelt (after the murder of Abel) was on the east of Eden.

A river went out and watered the garden. After passing the limits of Eden, the river is said to have divided itself, or parted, into four heads, i.e., arms or branches. The first branch was called Pison. This branch "compasseth," i.e., forms the boundary along the whole length of, "*the* Havilah." This country is spoken of as being a tract wherein was produced good gold, "b'dolach" (translated "bdellium") and "shoham" (translated "onyx.") The second branch was Gihon, which is described as similarly compassing the district of K[=u]sh. Here our A.V., by substituting "Ethiopia" for the original "C[=u]sh," has made a gloss rather than a translation; and this gloss has given rise to several errors of commentators in identifying the site of Eden. The Revised Version has corrected the error.

The third branch was Hiddekel, the *Diklatu* of the Arabs, the Tigra of the old Persians, and the *Tigris* of later writers. This is said to run eastward towards Assyria.[1] The fourth river was the Frat or Euphrates. Observe, in passing, that the author gives no detail about the great river Euphrates, as being well known; while he adds particulars about the Tigris, and describes the Gihon and the Pison in some detail.

It is in the identification of these two, and of the districts which they "compassed," which form the difficulties of the problem. Up till recent times, it is remarkable what a variety of speculations have been attempted as to the situation of Eden. Dr. Aldis Wright, the learned author of the article "Eden" in Smith's "Biblical Dictionary," remarks: "It would be difficult, in the whole history of opinion, to find any subject which has so invited, and at the same time completely baffled, conjecture, as the Garden of Eden." And in another place he thinks that "the site of Eden will ever rank with the quadrature of the circle, and the interpretation of unfulfilled prophecy among those unsolved, and perhaps insoluble, problems which possess so strange a fascination." It is, however, to be remarked, (1)that all that was written before Professor Delitzsch's researches were made known; and (2)that really a great mass of the conjecture and speculation has been purely in the air - undertaken without any reference to the plain terms of the text to be interpreted. It is the extravagance of commentators, and their insisting on going beyond the narrative itself, that has raised such difficulties, and made the problem look more hopeless than it really is.

To what purpose are "the three continents of the old world" "subjected to the most rigorous search," as Dr. Wright puts it - when it is quite plain from the text itself, that the solution is to be sought in the neighbourhood of the Euphrates, or not at all? The whole inquiry seems to have been one in which a vast cloud of learned dust has been raised by speculators, who began their inquiry without clearly determining, to start with, what was the point at issue. Either the description in Gen. ii. 3-14 is meant for allegory, or geographical fact: this question must first be settled; and if the latter is agreed to, then it is quite inconceivable that the words should imply any very extensive region, or any fancied realm extending over a large proportion of one or other quarter of the globe. The problem is then at once narrowed; and it is simply unreasonable to look for Havila in India, or for Pison in the province of Burma, as one learned author does!

Yet commentators have forgotten this; and gone - the earlier ones into interpretation of allegory - the later into impossible geographical speculation; while only the most recent have confined themselves to the obvious terms of the problem as laid down in the narrative itself - a narrative which (whether true or false) is clearly meant to be definite and exact, as we have seen. Our A.V. translators are to be held, to some extent, responsible for the freedom which speculation has exercised, by themselves taking the C[=u]sh of the narrative to "Ethiopia," i.e., to the African continent - for which there is no authority whatever.

As regards the *allegorical* interpretations, they are too extravagant for serious notice. Souls, angels, human passions and motives, are supposed to be represented by towns, rivers, and countries. To all this it is enough to reply - What reason can we have for supposing an allegory suddenly to be interpolated at Gen. ii. 8? There is no allegory before it, there is none after.

Then as to the early geographical expounders. Josephus and others supposed the allusion was made to the great rivers known to ancient geography, all of which ran into that greatest river of all, which encircled the globe. In this view, the Gihon might be the Nile, and the Pison the Ganges! Here, again, it may be remarked it is impossible to read the narrative and believe that the author meant any such widespread region. Even if the author had the ancient ideas about cosmography generally, that would not prevent his being accurate about a limited region lying to the east of a well-known river in a populous country. In later times Luther avoided the difficult speculation by supposing that the Deluge had swept away all traces of the site! But unfortunately for this convenient theory, it is a plain fact that the Deluge did not sweep any two out of the four rivers named. The reader who is curious on the subject, will find in Dr. A. Wright's article a brief account of the various identifications proposed by all these commentators. It would not be interesting to go into any detail. I shall pass over all those extravagant views which go to places remote from the Euphrates, and come at once to the later attempts to solve the question in connection with the two known rivers, Euphrates and Hiddekel (Tigris); as this is the only kind of solution that any reasonable modern Biblical student will admit.

The different explanations adopted maybe grouped into two main attempts: (1) to find the place among the group of rivers that surrounds Mount Ararat in Northern Armenia, *vis.*, in the extreme upper course of the Euphrates near its two sources; (2) to find the place below the *present* junction of the Euphrates and the Tigris, along some part of the united course, which is now more than two hundred miles long, and is called "Shatt-el-'Arab."

But neither of these attempts has been successful: the first must, indeed, be absolutely dismissed; because the Hebrew phrases used in describing the four *branches* of the river that "went out," and watered the garden, and then parted, cannot be applied to four independent sources or streams - *upstream* of the Euphrates. It will not, then, satisfy the problem, to find four rivers somewhere in the vicinity of the Euphrates, and which, in a general way, enclose a district in which Eden might be placed. It may, indeed, be doubted whether this first attempt (which I may call the "North Armenian solution") would ever have been seriously entertained, but from the fact that the name Gihon - or something very like it - did attach itself to the Araxes or Phasis, a considerable river of Armenia. Finding a Gihon ready, the commentators next made the Pison, the Acampsis; and then as Pison was near the "Havila land," this country was laid on the extreme north of Armenia; all this without a particle of evidence of any kind.[1] I may here take the opportunity of remarking that a chance *similarity of names*[2] has been, throughout the controversy, a fruitful source of enlarged speculative wandering. Thus this name Gihon (Gaihun, Jikhun, G[=e][=o]n, &c.) that appears in North Armenia, again appears in connection with the *Nile*; while again the name "Nile" has wandered back to the confines of Persia, and one of the *Euphrates* branches is still called "Shatt-en-nil." The ancients, indeed, had very curious ideas about the Nile. Its real sources being so long undiscovered - no Speke or Grant having appeared - imagination ran wild on the subject. Not only so, but it is remarkable that the name *Cush* should have acquired both a Persian Gulf and an Egyptian employment: and the writer of the able article in "The Nineteenth Century" (October, 1882) points out several other singular instances in which names are common both to the African-Egyptian region, and to this.

Turning now to the second of the two theories, the identification of the site on the lower part of the Euphrates after its now existing junction with the Tigris (and which the supporters of the theory have justified by making the Gihon and Pison two rivers coming from Eden) must also be set aside.

For the important fact has been overlooked that it is quite certain, that anciently, the joint stream, (Shatt-el-'Arab), as it now is, did not exist. Though the Genesis narrative tells us of a junction *immediately outside* the southern boundary of the Garden, the Euphrates channels and the Tigris branch (with part of the Euphrates water in it) flowed separately to the Persian Gulf. It is quite certain that, in the time of Alexander the Great, the mouths of the Euphrates and Tigris were a good day's journey apart. For this separate outflow there is the incontestable evidence of Pliny and other authors quoted by Professor Delitzsch. I may here also remark, that anciently the Persian Gulf extended much farther inland than it does now. In the time of Sennacherib, an inland arm of the sea extended so far, that a *naval* expedition against Elam was possible; more than one hundred miles inland from the present sea-line. The extension was called N[=a]r Marratum. In Alexander's time, the city of Charax (now Mohamra) was founded close to the sea (that was in the fourth century B.C.). It is known from later histories, that shortly before the birth of our Saviour, the city was from fifty to one hundred and twenty Roman miles inland. The change is due to the "Delta," or alluvial formation at the mouth of the rivers.

Turning, then, to the recent inquiries (published in 1881[1]) by Professor Fried. Delitzsch, it must be confessed that the results obtained are such as to completely avoid all the difficulties that beset the other explanations: yet we ought not to be too confident that it is a final or absolute explanation. A certain caution and reserve will still be wisely maintained on the subject. At any rate, they show that *an* explanation, one that answers *all* the conditions of the problem, *can* be given; and that is a great thing.

In placing the site *on* the Euphrates, and far from the mountain sources, there is no violence done to the Hebrew language used to describe the first river, as one that "went out," and watered the Garden. The words do not require that the river should actually *take* its *rise* within the Garden limits; but it is necessary that the river should be so situated, that its waters could be distributed by means of creeks or canals across the Garden, that it could be said the river "went out and watered the Garden." Now it is a remarkable fact, that in the district just above Babylon, the bed of the Euphrates is in level much higher than the bed of the Tigris (Hiddekel) to the east, and that hence there always have been a number of very variable channels leading from the Euphrates eastward to the Tigris. These, it is well known, were often enlarged by the ancients and converted into useful "inundation canals" for irrigation and the passage of boats. Imagine, then, the high level river bed of the Euphrates, and various streams flowing off it down to the valley of the Tigris, and we have a most efficiently irrigated "Garden," and one accurately described by the text - the great river "went out" and watered it. The Euphrates, moreover, is liable to great flushes of water from the melting of the snows in wide tracts of mountain or highlands from which its waters are collected, and these volumes of water found vent from the overcharged mother-channel by escape, not only through the side channels, just spoken of, but also by other important branches on the other side. Every one who has seen one of the great rivers of Northern India will at once realize the changes that take place where a river liable to floods has its bed at a high level. It is almost a matter of certainty that, in the course of years, the branches and channels of rivers so constituted will change, and old ones be left dry and deserted. These essential topographical conditions have always to be remembered in interpreting the narrative of Genesis ii.

In fact, they furnish us with points which help us in the problem at the outset. (1) There is a part of the Euphrates, just above Babylon, where the river naturally furnished abundant irrigation for a Garden planted eastward of it, by means of natural irrigation channels flowing from the high level down to the lower valley of the Tigris; and (2) there is also a point from which the Euphrates did branch out, and several important arms anciently existed.

Nor is the locality, in point of verdure and fertility, unsuitable. Not only do the ancient histories make frequent mention of the canals and streams flowing from the Euphrates which I have alluded to, but they speak of the palm groves, the vines and the verdure of the Babylonian or Chaldean region. Herodotus, in his first book, has the most glowing description of the scene; and the kings of Babylon had numerous enclosed gardens or parks: these were imitated in Persia, and gave rise to the Persian name "Firdaus," which Xenophon imported into Greek in the form of [Greek: paradeisos] or "paradise" - the term which was adopted by the Seventy translators.

The actual locality which Professor Delitzsch proposes as the most probable site of the Garden of Eden is between the present Euphrates and Tigris, just to the north of Babylon. The boundaries would be - roughly and generally speaking - the two rivers for East and West; while for the North and South boundaries we should draw parallel lines through Accad on the North and Babylon on the South.

But granted that the general locality and the relations of the river Euphrates and Tigris satisfy the requirements of the text by such a location as this: how about the other two *and* the countries which they compass? The troubles of the earlier commentators will warn us, that we need not be too ready to force names, and to identify one river, and then, *because* we have fixed that, make the country which the text requires follow it!

It is, however, in this matter that Professor Delitzsch's work is so satisfactory. He has pointed out, that there is historical evidence (and also that the local traces are not wanting in the present day) to prove that, just below Babylon, we *can* find two prominently important channels or branches of the Euphrates, which will at least supply the place of Pison and Gihon. As to the first, it is known that in historic times a great channel called by the Greeks Pallakopas (navigable for ships) used to carry off the surplus water of the Euphrates when swollen in the summer season by the melting snows of the Armenian mountains. It branched off from the main river at a point somewhat north of Babylon, and flowed into the Persian gulf. There is, indeed, no *direct* evidence to show that this branch bore a name resembling Pison. *Palgu* is the Assyrian whence the Greek Pallakopas was derived. It is remarkable, however, that the word Pison closely resembles the cuneiform term "pisana," or "pisanu," which is used for a water-reservoir, a canal or a channel; and as this "Pallakopas" was *the* channel *par excellence*, it may very possibly have been called "pisana" or Pison, the (great) channel. The identification of the channel called "Pallakopas" will be found mentioned in Colonel Chesney's work, "An Expedition to the Tigris." The name, however, of this channel is not the only means we have of identifying it. The Scripture says that the Pison compasses the land of *Havilah*. Now let us remember, that the Scripture tells of two Havilahs: (1) The second son of Cush[1] and brother of Nimrod, and (2) one of the great great grandsons of Shem (Gen. x. 29). One we may call the Cushite Havilah, the other the Joktanite Havilah. The dwelling-place of the brother of Nimrod is not mentioned, but it is stated that the Joktanite Havilah dwelt in "Mesha." The tenth of Genesis is an important chapter, as showing how the descendants of Noah branched out and spread over the countries all round the Euphrates; some going north to Assyria (Nineveh), others to the east and west, and others south, to Arabia and Egypt. Now it so happens that the whole country west of the great Pallakopas channel, was called by the Assyrians "Mashu." Professor Delitzsch identifies this Mashu of the cuneiform inscriptions, with the "Mesha" mentioned in Scriptures, as the home of Havilah. We have also in Gen. xxv. 8,[2] mention of a land of Havila that is "before" - i.e., eastward of - "Egypt as thou goest toward Assyria," which would answer very well to this locality, west of the Euphrates. It is also known (from sources which it would take too long to detail) that this country did yield gold-dust. Pliny also mentions "Bdellium," if that was the substance known as "B'dolach." It is indeed uncertain what this was, but Gesenius long ago rejected the idea that it was a stone, because there is no prefix to it, as there is to "shoham," which follows, and certainly is a precious stone. The manna in the wilderness is described as being of the "colour of bdellium," and was also like hoar-frost;[3] hence the idea that b'dolach was a crystal. But a fragrant and precious gum-resin seems more likely. The Magi who came to worship the Infant Saviour from near this locality, brought offerings of *gold*, and also fragrant gums and myrrh. Was "bdellium" (as probably being a fragrant gum) one of these offerings?

The "Onyx," or "Shoham," was most probably a pure red cornelian, and this also was found in the Babylonian provinces, and was specially worn by the Babylonian kings.

So the country west of the Euphrates answers very well to Havila without any forcing, and without any placing it there *because* of the river rendering such a plan necessary.

As to the fourth river (Gihon), Delitzsch identifies it, still more clearly, with a channel known as the "Shatten-nil," which branches off from the Euphrates at Babylon itself, and passing the Scriptural city of Erech, rejoins the main river lower down. A clay tablet has actually been discovered, having the Euphrates, Tigris, and this Shatt-en-nil channel *together*: the name of the latter is given as "K[=a]han de," or "Gughande," a name which closely resembles Gihon. The channel is, however, identified independently of the name. For the Gihon is particularized in the narrative, by the fact that it "compasses" the land of Cush. This (as already pointed out) is not the Ethiopian Cush.

Delitzsch states, that the whole country bounded by this branch was anciently called Kash-shu, which he identifies with the Cush of Genesis ii. The syllable "Kash" appears throughout this locality. In fact Kash-du or Kal-du is the origin of the familiar name Chaldea. In the Hebrew, Kush (Cush) is the name given to the father of Nimrod, who "began" his kingdom about this very site - Erech, and Calneh, and Accad (Gen. x. 8, 10). Hence it is not surprising that relics of the name should be found all round this neighbourhood. Nor does the evidence end here. The district immediately around Babylon was called "Kardunish-i," i.e., the "Garden of the god Dunish." Now Kar is the Turanian form of the Semitic G[=a]n, or Gin[=a] (garden); and what is more likely than that, as the true story was lost in the heathen traditions and mythology that grew up, the "garden" was attributed to the god Dunish - whereas the real original had been not "Gandunish," but "Gan'Eden?" This, though only a conjecture, is the more probable, as one of the inscription-names of Babylon itself was "Tintira," which, though a little obscure, certainly means *either* the "*grove*," or the *"fountain," of life*.

We thus find, not only that four great branches of the river that "went out," and watered the Garden can be traced, but that the two really do "compass" tracts, that can, with the highest degree of probability, be identified as C[=u]sh or Kash, and Havilah. The importance of Professor Delitzsch's work may now be briefly glanced at. It may be objected, that such a process of reasoning as that put forward, is not convincing to a general reader who has not the means of criticizing or testing Professor Delitzsch's conclusions: he therefore cannot be sure that, in selecting two channels to represent the Pison and the Gihon, and in identifying "Mashu" with Mesha of Havilah, and one of the Babylonian districts with Kush, the Professor has at last hit off a solution of the problem which will not in its turn be disproved, as all earlier solutions have been. There is, however, this important conclusion to be safely drawn, viz., that a complete explanation in exact accord with the Hebrew text is *possible*, and that hence nothing can be urged against the *narrative*, on the ground (hitherto sneeringly taken) that the geography *was impossible* and so forth.

Next let me very briefly sum up what it is that Dr. Delitzsch has done - marshalling the evidence, beginning from the broad end and narrowing down till we arrive at the point.

(1) First, then, we are fixed by the narrative to some place between the Euphrates and the Tigris.

(2) We find in the ancient inscriptions of the chief city of this locality, constant allusions to a Garden, a primitive pair and a temptation: one of these almost exactly reproduces the Bible story; it is not of the earliest date and is a copy. But discovery is far from being exhausted; all that we know is *consistent* with the idea of an original story, gradually corrupted by the addition of legends, and introduction of mythological persons and heathen divinities. The true belief in one God, who made Himself known by voice or vision to His true worshippers, seems early to have been confined to a few of the Shemitic families, while the others "invented" gods of their own.

(3) We find that the region about Babylon itself was called Kar-dunishi - which easily recalls Kar or Gan-Eden. We also find the name (Tintira) applied, indicating a "grove" or "fountain" of life; in the locality where the direct legends most abound.

(4) We find from ancient authors that the district was one of rich verdure - a land of gardens and irrigation.

(5) We find that some way above Babylon about Accad, the level of the river bed Euphrates is so much higher than the valley of the Tigris eastward, that

numerous streams flow off from it, which would serve admirably to irrigate a garden situated between the two, eastward of the Euphrates.

(6) We find that the Persian Gulf once extended more than one hundred miles farther inland than it does now. That there was no joint outflow of Tigris and Euphrates, but, though they did join their streams above, they parted again and had still separate mouths - of the Tigris branch one, of the Euphrates several.

(7) Lastly, Professor Delitzsch finds two channels which answer to Pison and Gihon.

(8) He proves these two to be the right ones by considering the countries which they "compass:" and actually finds the one that he supposes to be the "Gaihun," called, in the cuneiform clay tablets, "Kahan or Gaghan-de."

It is really only in (7) and (8) that there is any room for doubt and for further inquiry.

At any rate, the credibility of the narrative, and a belief in its purpose, as a topographically exact statement of fact, not an allegory or legend, is established.

Choose from Thousands of 1stWorldLibrary Classics By

Adolphus WilliamWard
Aesop
Agatha Christie
Alexander Aaronsohn
Alexander Kielland
Alexandre Dumas
Alfred Gatty
Alfred Ollivant
Alice Duer Miller
Alice Turner Curtis
Alice Dunbar
Ambrose Bierce
Amelia E. Barr
Andrew Lang
Andrew McFarland Davis
Anna Sewell
Annie Besant
Annie Hamilton Donnell
Annie Payson Call
Anton Chekhov
Arnold Bennett
Arthur Conan Doyle
Arthur Ransome
Atticus
B. M. Bower
Basil King
Bayard Taylor
Ben Macomber
Booth Tarkington
Bram Stoker
C. Collodi
C. E. Orr
C. M. Ingleby
Carolyn Wells
Catherine Parr Traill
Charles A. Eastman
Charles Dickens
Charles Dudley Warner
Charles Farrar Browne
Charles Ives
Charles Kingsley
Charles Lathrop Pack
Charles Whibley
Charles Willing Beale
Charlotte M. Braeme
Charlotte M.Yonge
Clair W. Hayes
Clarence Day Jr.
Clarence E. Mulford

Clemence Housman
Confucius
Cornelis DeWitt Wilcox
Cyril Burleigh
D. H. Lawrence
Daniel Defoe
David Garnett
Don Carlos Janes
Donald Keyhole
Dorothy Kilner
Dougan Clark
E. Nesbit
E.P.Roe
E. Phillips Oppenheim
Edgar Allan Poe
Edgar Rice Burroughs
Edith Wharton
Edward J. O'Biren
John Cournos
Edwin L. Arnold
Eleanor Atkins
Elizabeth Cleghorn
Gaskell
Elizabeth Von Arnim
Ellem Key
Emily Dickinson
Erasmus W. Jones
Ernie Howard Pie
Ethel Turner
Ethel Watts Mumford
Eugenie Foa
Eugene Wood
Evelyn Everett-Green
Everard Cotes
F. J. Cross
Federick Austin Ogg
Ferdinand Ossendowski
Francis Bacon
Francis Darwin
Frances Hodgson Burnett
Frank Gee Patchin
Frank Harris
Frank Jewett Mather
Frank L. Packard
Frederick Trevor Hill
Frederick Winslow Taylor
Friedrich Kerst
Friedrich Nietzsche
Fyodor Dostoyevsky

Gabrielle E. Jackson
Garrett P. Serviss
Gaston Leroux
George Ade
Geroge Bernard Shaw
George Ebers
George Eliot
George MacDonald
George Orwell
George Tucker
George W. Cable
George Wharton James
Gertrude Atherton
Grace E. King
Grant Allen
Guillermo A. Sherwell
Gulielma Zollinger
Gustav Flaubert
H. A. Cody
H. B. Irving
H. G. Wells
H. H. Munro
H. Irving Hancock
H. Rider Haggard
H. W. C. Davis
Hamilton Wright Mabie
Hans Christian Andersen
Harold Avery
Harold McGrath
Harriet Beecher Stowe
Harry Houidini
Helent Hunt Jackson
Helen Nicolay
Hendy David Thoreau
Henrik Ibsen
Henry Adams
Henry Ford
Henry Frost
Henry James
Henry Jones Ford
Henry Seton Merriman
Henry Wadsworth
Longfellow
Henry W Longfellow
Herbert A. Giles
Herbert N. Casson
Herman Hesse
Homer
Honore De Balzac

Horace Walpole
Horatio Alger, Jr.
Howard Pyle
Howard R. Garis
Hugh Lofting
Hugh Walpole
Humphry Ward
Ian Maclaren
Israel Abrahams
J.G.Austin
J. Henri Fabre
J. M. Barrie
J. Macdonald Oxley
J. S. Knowles
J. Storer Clouston
Jack London
Jacob Abbott
James Allen
James Lane Allen
James Andrews
James Baldwin
James DeMille
James Joyce
James Oliver Curwood
James Oppenheim
James Otis
Jane Austen
Jens Peter Jacobsen
Jerome K. Jerome
John Burroughs
John F. Kennedy
John Gay
John Glasworthy
John Habberton
John Joy Bell
John Milton
John Philip Sousa
Jonathan Swift
Joseph Carey
Joseph Conrad
Joseph Jacobs
Julian Hawthrone
Julies Vernes
Justin Huntly McCarthy
Kakuzo Okakura
Kenneth Grahame
Kate Langley Bosher
L. A. Abbot
L. T. Meade
L. Frank Baum
Laura Lee Hope

Laurence Housman
Leo Tolstoy
Leonid Andreyev
Lewis Carroll
Lilian Bell
Lloyd Osbourne
Louis Tracy
Louisa May Alcott
Lucy Fitch Perkins
Lucy Maud Montgomery
Lydia Miller Middleton
Lyndon Orr
M. H. Adams
Margaret E. Sangster
Margaret Vandercook
Maria Edgeworth
Maria Thompson Daviess
Mariano Azuela
Marion Polk Angellotti
Mark Overton
Mark Twain
Mary Austin
Mary Cole
Mary Rowlandson
Mary Wollstonecraft
Shelley
Max Beerbohm
Myra Kelly
Nathaniel Hawthrone
O. F. Walton
Oscar Wilde
Owen Johnson
P.G.Wodehouse
Paul and Mable Thorn
Paul G. Tomlinson
Paul Severing
Peter B. Kyne
Plato
R. Derby Holmes
R. L. Stevenson
Rabindranath Tagore
Rahul Alvares
Ralph Waldo Emmerson
Rene Descartes
Rex E. Beach
Richard Harding Davis
Richard Jefferies
Robert Barr
Robert Frost
Robert Gordon Anderson
Robert L. Drake

Robert Lansing
Robert Michael Ballantyne
Robert W. Chambers
Rosa Nouchette Carey
Ross Kay
Rudyard Kipling
Samuel B. Allison
Samuel Hopkins Adams
Sarah Bernhardt
Selma Lagerlof
Sherwood Anderson
Sigmund Freud
Standish O'Grady
Stanley Weyman
Stella Benson
Stephen Crane
Stewart Edward White
Stijn Streuvels
Swami Abhedananda
Swami Parmananda
T. S. Ackland
The Princess Der Ling
Thomas A. Janvier
Thomas A Kempis
Thomas Anderton
Thomas Bailey Aldrich
Thomas Bulfinch
Thomas De Quincey
Thomas H. Huxley
Thomas Hardy
Thomas More
Thornton W. Burgess
U. S. Grant
Valentine Williams
Victor Appleton
Virginia Woolf
Walter Scott
Washington Irving
Wilbur Lawton
Wilkie Collins
Willa Cather
Willard F. Baker
William Makepeace
Thackeray
William W. Walter
Winston Churchill
Yei Theodora Ozaki
Young E. Allison
Zane Grey

www.ingramcontent.com/pod-product-compliance
Lightning Source LLC
Chambersburg PA
CBHW051754040426
42446CB00007B/360